Foreword

Electronic monitoring is a relatively new development in the field of criminal justice. Its growth has been rapid in the USA and it is also in use in Canada and Australia. A trial project to test out the feasibility of electronic monitoring in England and Wales began in August 1989 at three locations—Nottingham, North Tyneside, and Tower Bridge in London—and concluded earlier this year. The target population was defendants who, in the absence of electronic monitoring, would have been remanded in custody. This report provides a full account of the monitoring project: it looks at the organisation and operation of the trials, sets out the results of monitoring, and discusses the views of some of those who were bailed subject to a condition of electronic monitoring. The report concludes by pointing to issues raised by the trial which should help to inform any further initiatives in this area.

ROGER TARLING

Head of the Research and Planning Unit

Acknowledgements

Without the co-operation and assistance of a great many people in each of the three trial areas this research would not have been possible. We are particularly grateful to Beth Henderson, Barry Hill and Chief Inspector Chris Bartle in Nottingham; David Greensmith, Stan Sudworth and Chief Inspector Marjorie Milner in North Tyneside; and Caroline Tubbs and Chief Superintendent Alan Evershed in Tower Bridge. Thanks are also due to the Marconi and Chubb operatives in each of the three sites, especially Keith Taylor and John Le Bentz; and to all those defendants who agreed to be interviewed about their experiences with electronic monitoring. Finally, we wish to thank Margaret Ayres, Richard Brett, Neil Clowes, Simon Field and Moya Lenaghan.

GEORGE MAIR
CLAIRE NEE

HOME OFFICE RES

Electronic Monitoring: The Trials and Their Results

by George Mair and Claire Nee
with the assistance of Gordon Barclay and
Keith Wickham

A HOME OFFICE
RESEARCH AND PLANNING UNIT
REPORT

LONDON: HMSO

First published 1990

ISBN 0 11 340998 2

HOME OFFICE RESEARCH STUDIES

'Home Office Research Studies' comprise reports on research undertaken in the Home Office to assist in the exercise of its administrative functions, and for the information of the judicature, the services for which the Home Secretary has responsibility (direct or indirect) and the general public.

On the last page of this report are listed titles already published in this series, in the preceding series Studies in the Causes of Delinquency and the Treatment of Offenders, and in the series of Research and Planning Unit Papers.

HMSO

Standing order service

Placing a standing order with HMSO BOOKS enables a customer to receive other titles in this series automatically as published.

This saves time, trouble and expense of placing individual orders and avoids the problem of knowing when to do so.

For details please write to HMSO BOOKS (PC13A/1), Publications centre, P.O. Box 276, London SW8 5DT and quoting reference 25.08.011.

The standing order service also enables customers to receive automatically as published all material of their choice which additionally saves extensive catalogue research. The scope and selectivity of the service has been extended by new techniques, and there are more than 3,500 classifications to chose from. A special leaflet describing the service in detail may be obtained on request.

Contents

1 Introduction

Although it is still too soon to be certain of its lasting significance, one of the key developments in penal policy during the 1980s has undoubtedly been the use of electronic surveillance techniques to monitor the whereabouts of defendants and offenders. First used in the U.S.A., electronic monitoring is now in use in Australia and Canada. A trial project to test the general feasibility of electronic monitoring in England and Wales began in August 1989, and a research project was set up to evaluate the trial. This report describes the organisation of the trial, sets out the findings of the research, and assesses how far the initiative was successful.

While on the one hand electronic monitoring may be seen as simply another step in the search for an effective and economic method of diverting offenders and defendants from custody, from another point of view it is perceived as a radical break with the penal past. Similarly, electronic monitoring is often seen as a brand-new approach to dealing with offenders, but conversely monitoring is only a tool whereby one of the oldest means of dealing with criminals—home detention or house arrest (see Lilly and Ball 1987)—can be policed more efficiently and effectively. To add to the debate, electronic monitoring is also a step in what might be perceived as the privatisation of the penal system. The use of electronic monitoring has, therefore, been subject to a good deal of controversy. Unfortunately, the nature of the claims and counter-claims made by supporters and detractors of electronic monitoring have not clarified the key issues and may, indeed, have served only to confuse them.

In the U.S.A. the need to sell (literally) electronic monitoring has led to the aggressive marketing of competing devices with consequent claims about effectiveness which have not been substantiated. The pressures faced by those working in the penal system to cut overcrowding in prisons, to do this with regard to public safety, and at the same time to take account of financial costs has led officials to grab at anything which might help them solve these problems. Electronic monitoring has, to a great extent, been accepted uncritically as the solution to these problems. Thus, large sums of money have been invested in equipment, monitoring programmes have been set up and the success of schemes has been asserted; too much time and money have been invested for anything less to be acceptable. For the most part, research has not helped to dissipate the confusion. A substantial amount has been written on electronic monitoring during the last five years, but the quality of much of the research has been poor. Too many researchers have been rushing to study programmes which are in their infancy, and where very few people have been monitored. Outcome measures are used to assess the success of programmes before they have settled down, and there is little acknowledgement of the methodological difficulties involved.

The situation in England and Wales has been rather different. While there have been a few signs of aggressive marketing these have been held in check by the centralised nature of penal decision-making. Thus, instead of many different programmes developing with no central control as in the U.S.A., one set of trials was set up which would run in three different locations. The trials were run by the Home Office and it was agreed that they would be the subject of research by the Research and Planning Unit with assistance from Statistical Department and the Scientific Research and Development Branch. The formal objectives of the trials were fourfold:

i. to evaluate the extent to which the availability of electronic monitoring can enable defendants to be remanded on bail rather than in custody;

ii. to evaluate current electronic monitoring technology;

iii. to evaluate the cost-effectiveness, and appropriateness of privatising electronic monitoring; and

iv. to inform consideration of the scope for widening the application of electronic monitoring to sentenced offenders who would otherwise receive custodial sentences

Chapter 2 of this report sets out the background to the trials and includes a brief review of the literature on electronic monitoring. Chapter 3 describes the planning for the trials and the types of equipment used. In Chapter 4 an account is presented of the progress of the trial in each of its three locations. Chapter 5 provides the results of the trials in terms of the numbers monitored, curfew hours, failure rates and so on. Chapter 6 reports the results of interviews with those who were subject to electronic monitoring, while Chapter 7 gives an assessment of the performance of the equipment. Finally, Chapter 8 attempts to pull together the key points emerging from the trials and to draw some conclusions.

2 Background to the trials

This is not the place for a full analysis of the origins of the decision to carry out a trial of electronic monitoring, but a brief outline of some of the issues which contributed to the decision will help to contextualise the initiative. Several key factors can be identified, although no attempt will be made to weight their significance.

The first point is, of course, the existence of electronic monitoring as a criminal justice tool in the U.S.A. New practices in penology, as is the case in other areas of policy, do not necessarily remain confined to one geographical area. We usually assume that ideas and practices from North America tend to move across the Atlantic and become embedded in Britain, but this is by no means always the case and movement in the other direction is quite possible; in the penal field, community service and day centres are two examples of initial developments in England and Wales which have been adopted in the U.S.A. (and certainly in the case of community service in many other countries also). With regard to electronic monitoring, however, the movement has been from North America to England and Wales. The Home Office does not operate in splendid isolation and both administrators and researchers were aware of the developments in electronic monitoring in the U.S.A. by the mid-eighties. The subject was further encouraged in various ways: the manufacturers of monitoring equipment were eager to demonstrate their wares to Home Office officials; a one-day conference on electronic monitoring in Canada was held in London in October 1987; and the Offenders' Tag Association (a British pressure group) was not slow in making representations to the Home Office. It is not surprising, then, that electronic monitoring took its place on the penal policy agenda.

But a policy without a problem to tackle is not likely to make much progress. Crucial to the adoption of electronic monitoring was the continuing existence of serious custodial overcrowding. The average custodial population in 1987 was 49,000—an excess of 7,000 over the certified normal accommodation (Home Office 1988a), and an increase of 2,000 over the previous year. Moreover, more than 20 per cent of that population was made up of prisoners on remand who had not been tried or had not been sentenced; a proportion which had increased each year from 17 per cent in 1982. Furthermore, during 1987 an average of 540 people were held in police cells (which are several times more expensive than prison), the great majority of whom were unsentenced. Thus, as was very much the case in the U.S.A., electronic monitoring was seen as a means of tackling prison overcrowding.

In March 1987, the House of Commons Home Affairs Committee in a report on the *State and Use of Prisons* recommended that 'the Home Office should study the use made of electronic tagging of offenders in the U.S.A. to see what, if any, application it has in England and Wales' (House of Commons 1987). Later in the same year a Home Office Minister of State, Lord Caithness, visited electronic monitoring projects in the course of a visit to the U.S.A. By 1987 preparations were underway in the Home Office for a serious re-think of penal policy and in July 1988 *Punishment, Custody and the Community* (Home Office 1988b) was published. In the discussion part of this Green Paper the possibility was raised of using electronic monitoring

> . . . to enforce tracking or an order requiring the offender to stay at home for a limited period, thereby making it possible to keep out of custody offenders who would otherwise be in prison.

By the middle of 1988 it had been decided to set up an electronic monitoring experiment in England and Wales. Before describing the detailed planning which was necessary for the trials (see Chapter 3), it will be helpful to survey briefly the American literature on electronic monitoring.

Electronic Monitoring—the American experience

While an initial flurry of interest in the use of electronic monitoring in the area of corrections was created by the work of Schwitzgebel and his colleagues in the 1960s (see Gable 1986), for our purposes electronic monitoring can be said to have begun in 1983. This was when Judge Jack Love in New Mexico, inspired by a *Spiderman* comic strip, encouraged the design of a monitoring system and subsequently used it on offenders. Since then, the use of electronic monitoring in the criminal justice system has grown exponentially, which may—on the face of it—be seen as proof of its success and is certainly taken to be so by manufacturers of monitoring equipment. A considerable literature—much of it unpublished—has arisen around the subject of electronic monitoring, but only the more important examples will be discussed in this brief review.

The first papers on electronic monitoring, not surprisingly, discussed issues surrounding the use of monitoring as no data were available on programmes. Thus Houk (1984) discussed the potential intrusiveness of electronic monitoring before and after conviction, and argued that if it was to be used in conjunction with probation it should be related to the specific aims of the probation order. Berry (1985) too noted the constitutional issues—particularly the right to privacy—surrounding electronic monitoring, and pointed out that monitoring might be used for various populations; as an add-on to probation, for pre-trial release, work release, early or temporary release from prison, or to monitor certain groups in prison. She emphasised the potential for net-widening:

> Above all, the danger of widening the correctional net should be considered. The availability of a new device should not be a reason

> for using it in unjustified situations. Specifically, we must be cautious about using this correctional strategy on persons who would not normally be included. (Berry 1985)

And this warning is echoed by Sullivan and Alpert (1986), who also make the point that electronic monitoring is not an alternative to custody by itself but a technological method which can enhance existing alternatives so that they may become more effective alternatives to custody.

The constitutional and legal issues were addressed again by del Carmen and Vaughn (1986) who concluded that

> . . . the constitutionality of the use of electronic devices in probation is strongly defensible. Whether or not such use is cost-effective, politically acceptable, or administratively feasible is an entirely different matter.

And Annesley Schmidt (1986), of the National Institute of Justice, listed a series of questions about electronic monitoring which remained without answers: for what kind of offenders and programmes is monitoring most effective; what kind of equipment should be used and how does this affect the structure of programmes; for how long should offenders be monitored; does net-widening result; how much does monitoring cost? Technological problems with equipment were also noted. The one question to which Schmidt did offer an answer was whether or not electronic monitoring could alleviate prison overcrowding—and the response was that it would probably not do so.

An early report on an electronic monitoring programme in Kenton County, Kentucky was produced by Lilly and Wright (1986). This concluded that electronic monitoring had been 'more than a modest success', although the basis for this conclusion is rather weak. The home incarceration programme did not significantly reduce jail overcrowding; although it is claimed that all of those included in the programme were alternatives to custody. This latter claim, however, is not based on any real evidence apart from the fact that all of those monitored could have been sent to jail, and that the three judges involved indicated that they might indeed have sentenced some of the offenders to jail. Judges were in favour of the programme, but used it conservatively. A rather simplistic comparison of the financial costs of electronic monitoring and of imprisonment shows that the latter is cheaper, but it is claimed that over time as more and more people are sentenced to home incarceration with monitoring 'the cost comparisons with jail time will reverse'. The major problem with the research is that it is based on only 23 offenders who were monitored during the first six months of the programme's existence. Subsequent reports on the same programme with 35 offenders (Lilly, Ball and Wright 1987) and with 39 offenders (Ball, Huff and Lilly 1988) make the same claims, but no more convincingly.

Jolin (1987) studied the Clackamas County, Oregon electronic surveillance programme which was located in the probation department but took referrals from a variety of sources. The programme used two methods of monitoring, an active and a passive system, with the passive proving to be more successful because of the large number of equipment faults which occurred with the active system (which was a radio frequency system). Ninety-six offenders were placed on the programme in the first year and 86 of these completed successfully their period of monitoring (an average of 33 days per offender). Because the programme was in its infancy 'few guidelines remained constant during the first seven months' and this made full evaluation impossible. It is interesting to note, however, that having a relatively stable work situation was one of the few firm criteria for acceptance on to the programme. Family members of those subject to monitoring were fairly positive about the experience.

A pilot project in Washtenaw County, Michigan using electronic monitoring as a sentence of the court which would function as an alternative to custody aimed for at least 20 offenders in the first six months, but could only manage to identify 12 offenders (Hatchett 1987). There were problems with the equipment although these diminished during the course of the project. The criteria for accepting participants for monitoring were clear and seem to have been adhered to, and this would appear to be the major reason for the low number of offenders monitored. Despite this, those monitored had less serious criminal histories than those considered for monitoring but sentenced to custody; and this casts some doubt upon the efficacy of monitoring acting as an alternative to custody. Most of those monitored complied with the programme conditions (which meant that there was little risk to the public), and of the successfully completed cases four were monitored for 90 days and four for 180 days.

A review of ten different electronic monitoring programmes carried out by the National Institute of Justice (Friel, Vaughn and del Carmen 1987) demonstrated the wide variety of monitoring programmes—pre-trial, as a sentence, and as a condition of early/work release from custody—and showed that most of the key questions remained unanswered. The kind of equipment used varied from area to area as did the size of the programme, its target group and eligibility criteria. The maximum duration of monitoring had been 311 days (in Palm Beach, Florida), while the average period of monitoring ranged from one month to four months. All of the programmes were voluntary. One key point which was stressed was the need for careful planning before electronic monitoring was introduced; this was essential in order to be certain of the nature of the problem, to consider various options for solving it, and to involve criminal justice agencies in the development of any initiatives. It was considered imperative that electronic monitoring was not seen crudely as a quick and easy solution to the problems of prison overcrowding. Mendelsohn and Baumer (1987) in a paper describing a programme in Marion County, Indiana point to a series of issues which had an impact upon the practical application of the programme; target slippage, the availability of telephones, the costs of the programme, curfew exceptions and problematic work schedules. Such issues make electronic monitoring programmes much more complicated than they may at first appear to be.

The need for some guidance for agencies which were planning to introduce electronic monitoring was recognised by the Bureau of Justice Assistance (1989). Because of the many possible uses of monitoring as a criminal justice tool, it is considered important to define specific programme objectives and target groups well in advance—and especially before discussing plans with vendors of equipment. The need for evaluation research to be included in the design of any monitoring programme is emphasised, and any evaluation should cover the implementation process as well as outcome measures. The relevance of such advice is underlined by the most detailed and careful study carried out so far into the use of electronic monitoring (Baumer and Mendelsohn 1990). They concluded that the use of electronic monitoring required a great deal of organisation and planning and should not be seen as an easy solution. Neither the rate of offender compliance with the rules of home detention nor the probability of further contact with the criminal justice system during a 12 month follow-up period differed according to whether the offender was monitored electronically or through personal contact.

In 1990 it is likely that the daily electronically monitored population in the U.S.A. will be in excess of 10,000 (Renzema and Skelton 1990). The growth of monitoring has been rapid in the last five years and there are now monitoring programmes in almost all of the States. Yet the evidence for the success of electronic monitoring as a criminal justice tool is, at best, equivocal. The reasons for its growth are essentially threefold: the level of prison and jail overcrowding, a loss of faith in the efficacy of probation, and a fiscal crisis which has made it very difficult to justify further expenditure. The appeal of electronic monitoring, and its acceptance by criminal justice agencies, lies in its perceived ability to tackle all three of these problems (an ability which is, of course, emphasised by equipment vendors). Within the next few years further, more reliable studies such as that carried out by Baumer and Mendelsohn (1990) should appear. Until then, the verdict on electronic monitoring in the U.S.A. will remain ‘not proven’.

3 Preparing for the trials

While the decision to test out electronic monitoring had been taken by the middle of 1988, it took 12 months involving a great deal of work before the first trial began in Nottingham. The introduction of electronic monitoring to the criminal justice system was not something which could be done casually and informally; systems to run the initiative in the field had to be planned and set up from scratch. In the event, 12 months was in fact a remarkably short time in which to carry out all the planning and detailed negotiations which had to be done before the trials commenced.

Having decided to try out electronic monitoring, the first question which had to be answered was who would be monitored. In the USA, as has been noted, electronic monitoring is used for a variety of populations: those who have not yet been convicted, as a condition of probation, as a sentence in its own right, and as a condition of early release from custody. It was clear from the beginning that monitoring could not legally be used as a sentence of the court; legislation would be necessary for this and the Parliamentary timetable was too busy to allow access for a new Bill to be presented at short notice. Legal advice made it clear that electronic monitoring would be possible under current legislation as a condition of bail for an unconvicted defendant or unsentenced offender. But the main interest in the use of monitoring lay in its claims to provide effective diversion from custody. Therefore, it was agreed that for the trials electronic monitoring would only be used for those who would otherwise have been remanded in custody; in other words, it was to be offered as an alternative to custody.

This decision opened the door to other problems. The bail/remand decision can involve all of the major agencies of the criminal justice system: the police, the Crown Prosecution Service, the courts, the probation service, and the prison service. By using electronic monitoring in this area it meant that all of these agencies might have to be involved in the planning of the trials. A second problem arising from the need to restrict monitoring to the bail/remand area was that this was a subject which was receiving considerable attention as a result of the size of the remand population (Stone 1988, Mair 1988). Bail information schemes run by the probation service were spreading rapidly across the country, and it was felt that the electronic monitoring trials should not be carried out in an area where such a scheme was in existence. It was agreed that monitoring should take place in relatively busy courts where large numbers of defendants were appearing for bail/remand decisions, but the growth of bail information schemes was planned to commence with the busiest courts and many courts which might have been considered for electronic monitoring had to be ruled out because of the presence of bail schemes.

It might have been an interesting experiment to make available electronic monitoring in an area where a bail information scheme was operating. In theory, the target for each initiative was different: those subject to electronic monitoring should be defendants who would otherwise have been remanded in custody; while those who were helped by bail schemes should be defendants who would have been bailed if the appropriate information had been known to the court. In practice, however, confusion would have been likely and this would not have helped the development of either bail information schemes or electronic monitoring.

It was considered essential to try electronic monitoring in more than one area, but resource constraints limited the trial period to six months in three petty sessional divisions. Taking all of these factors into consideration, several petty sessional divisions were approached about participating in the trials and after discussion three PSDs were chosen: Nottingham City, North Tyneside, and Tower Bridge (London).

Having decided upon a target population and chosen the three areas where the trials would take place, a series of meetings began with representatives of the criminal justice agencies from each area (essentially the police, justices' clerks, the Crown Prosecution Service, and Crown Court administrators) where Home Office officials outlined the nature of the trials and their objectives. At the same time, the details of the trials were being refined in the Home Office with a view to preparing a formal specification for companies to tender for the work involved in setting up a system to monitor electronically defendants on bail.

Basically, there are two types of electronic monitoring systems—continuously signalling, or 'active' systems, and programmed contact, or 'passive' systems. Programmed contact systems only verify a person's presence at a particular location at random times; usually, a computer generates random telephone calls to a residence during any curfew period and the person being monitored is required to answer and confirm his/her identity. This system does not monitor a person during the whole of a curfew period but only at random times during it; it is also likely to be more of an intrusion to those who live in the same household who might be annoyed by several telephone calls in the course of a night. The 'active' system, conversely, monitors an individual for the whole of any curfew period and a telephone call is only made where an infraction is suspected. It was decided from the beginning that for the trials it was the 'active' system which would be used. This system consists of three pieces of equipment: (1) a transmitter-bracelet which is worn on the wrist or leg and which sends out signals when it is within range of (2) a receiver-dialler attached to the telephone line which relays the signals to (3) a central computer which receives and stores these data, and warns any operator if a person is absent during any curfew period.

Again, this decision led to a series of other questions which had to be resolved before a formal request for tenders was sent out to interested companies. Would only one type of continuously signalling system be used? What should be the effective signal range of the transmitter? What size should the transmitter be? Should the transmitter bracelet include a tamper-proof device? How often should the equipment be checked? These are only a few of the questions which had to be answered; set out below are the key final specifications which were agreed for the transmitters which might be used during the trials.

1. The transmitter must be capable of being attached to the participant in such a manner that efforts to remove it or tamper with it in any way are detectable during the weekly equipment check.
2. For trial sites North Tyneside and Tower Bridge, the bracelet transmitter shall include a reliable, proven mechanism to indicate tampering of that device. Should tampering be detected the mechanism will cause the receiver/dialler to inform automatically the central computer.
3. The signal emitted by the transmitter shall not interfere with, or be affected by, any other equipment or external legal radio source(s) located in the vicinity of the participant's place of residence.
4. The transmitter shall be uniquely paired with the receiver/dialler situated in the participant's place of residence.
5. The effective signal range of the transmitter shall be adjustable to between 50 and 200 feet. A 15 per cent tolerance will be allowed. Four ranges are required—50, 100, 150 and 200 feet.
6. The transmitter should be battery powered with a minimum of three months between replacement/recharging.
7. The transmitter must emit a signal at least once every five minutes.
8. The transmitter shall be shock-resistant; waterproof to a depth of three metres; operate in a temperature range of -10 to 50 degrees centigrade and function reliably under average atmospheric and environmental conditions as experienced in the UK.
9. The transmitter must not pose a safety hazard nor unduly restrict the activities of the participant. It should be as small as possible, preferably less than 75mm × 65mm × 25mm and weigh less than 25 grams.

Similarly detailed specifications covered the receiver/dialler and the central computer.

Besides supplying the equipment and using it to monitor the presence/absence of participants in the trials, the contractors were to brief participants on the use of equipment, attach the transmitter to and remove it from participants, install and maintain the receiver/dialler in the participant's place of residence, arrange for the installation of a telephone in a participant's home if this was necessary (and arrange its removal when monitoring was complete), carry out checking procedures in the event of any alleged violation of bail, inform the police when a violation did occur, inspect the participant's equipment regularly, and liaise with the courts when taking on and releasing participants.

The criteria for deciding who might be subject to electronic monitoring were further refined. As well as being available as a condition of bail where the defendant would otherwise have been remanded in custody, defendants had to be volunteers, they had to be 17 or over (in other words, juveniles could not be included), they would have to reside in the area covered by the jurisdiction of the court and be likely to remain at the same address for the duration of the monitoring period. In addition, only defendants who were not likely to pose a danger to members of the public should be considered for monitoring; and where monitoring was to take place in a defendant's home, undue hardship should not be caused to the families of defendants or other occupants. Both male and female defendants would be considered for monitoring.

A key requirement for any participant in the monitoring programme was to have a telephone, or to agree to the installation of a telephone. Detailed negotiations had to be held with British Telecom over their agreement and ability to supply a telephone line where necessary within a reasonable amount of time after they had been alerted by the service suppliers that this would be necessary. In the event, British Telecom agreed to supply a telephone within 24 hours of being so requested, although serious difficulties would arise if there were no lines available in the area where a defendant lived—the cost and time needed in such cases would be prohibitive (defendants would have to be kept in custody while these arrangements were being made). Where telephones were supplied, these could not be used for outgoing calls by defendants and as the telephone number was not known to defendants, their friends could not keep the lines busy by ringing.

In the normal decision-making process about whether or not to oppose bail for those charged with an offence, the police simply divide cases into two groups—those for whom they would not oppose bail and those for whom they would (essentially, this latter group is being recommended for a remand in custody). For the purposes of the trials, the police agreed to modify this practice so that they would look again at those cases where they were opposing bail and, taking account of the guideline criteria as far as possible, make recommendations about those cases where they would not oppose bail if the defendant were to be subject to a condition of electronic monitoring. It should be noted that this procedure whereby decisions were to be reconsidered was somewhat artificial. Cases papers are then passed on to the Crown Prosecution Service (CPS) where a decision is made about whether or not to follow the police recommendation regarding bail, and specifically for the purposes of the trials whether or not to agree with any police recommendations for electronic monitoring. The CPS also agreed to give further consideration to possible cases where they themselves might recommend monitoring although the police had decided against.

When a CPS recommendation for electronic monitoring was made, the court officer would be informed who would in turn alert the service supplier that he might be required to fit a device. Ultimately, of course, the bail/remand decision is made by the magistrates in the light of all the circumstances surrounding the case and they were aware of the guideline criteria for electronic monitoring cases. Defence solicitors too could offer their clients for electronic monitoring, and the magistrates themselves could decide to grant bail subject to a condition of monitoring without any recommendation from the CPS or the defence.

Discussing the roles of the various agencies which would be involved in electronic monitoring took considerable time. Agreements which were reached with an agency might have to be amended in the light of the organisation of another, and detailed negotiations had to be carried out with regard to inter-agency liaison and communication. The three agencies directly involved in all of the planning were the police, the CPS and the court clerks. Efforts were made to keep magistrates and defence solicitors fully aware of the plans for the trials and the guideline criteria for electronic monitoring, but the sheer numbers of both these groups made it difficult to be certain that everyone was as well-informed as might be desirable. No detailed plans were made in advance for Crown Court involvement in the trials. While it was clear that judges in the three trial areas could make use of electronic monitoring in bail applications, it was considered to be advisable to decide on any formal procedures after Crown Court use of monitoring had occurred on a few occasions. Detailed planning was also not made in the case of prison involvement; where a defendant had to wait for a telephone to be installed before he/she could be monitored, a remand in custody might be necessary but this was assumed not to be problematic.

When a decision to monitor a defendant had been made, the agreement of the defendant to monitoring and to his/her proposed curfew hours had to be sought. Both the defendant and a representative of the service supplier would sign an *Electronic Monitoring Agreement* (see Appendix) which would set out the conditions. The transmitter would then be fitted by the service supplier and the defendant would be allowed a certain amount of time to return to his/her residence after which monitoring would begin. One of the critical issues which had to be resolved was the problem of alleged violations; when should a violation become notifiable and to whom should it be notified? Generally, violation procedures were divided into Level 1 violations (where the violation did not continue beyond two hours and a written report would be sent to the police, the CPS and the court the following day), and Level 2 violations where the police would be informed as soon as possible after two hours had elapsed and no longer than four hours after the violation had commenced (tamper alerts were dealt with as Level 2 violations). It was agreed that the response times for individual defendants could be varied where the police considered this to be necessary in the interests of public safety.

The first step in any alleged violation was to carry out a check of the computer, and then the defendant's telephone. If the fault was in the latter, then British Telecom would be informed. If faulty monitoring equipment was suspected the defendant would be visited for an equipment check. Whenever any alleged violation occurred, the objective of the service supplier was to re-establish contact with the defendant as quickly as possible. Each of the three trial areas received a different level of service on alleged violations: Nottingham used a non-tamper alert transmitter with a slow response from the suppliers; North Tyneside used a tamper alert transmitter with medium response from the suppliers; and Tower Bridge also used a tamper alert transmitter but with a fast response. The response time was based upon the number of operators in each area: in Nottingham, one person covered each eight hour shift and he was expected to go out and check on problems at defendants' residences as well as look after the central computer; the medium response in North Tyneside used two people during 9.00 a.m. and 5.00 p.m. and one person during the remainder of each day; while at Tower Bridge two people were on duty all of the time. In the event, there was no discernible difference in the effectiveness of responses to alleged violations amongst the three areas because of the low numbers of defendants monitored.

When the decision to try out electronic monitoring had been announced, a great many companies had expressed interest in supplying the equipment and carrying out the monitoring. A total of 60 companies intially were known to be interested, but only 36 expressed sufficient interest to be sent a letter and questionnaire; 15 companies returned these and a shortlist of six companies was drawn up and invited to tender. The contracts for the Nottingham and North Tyneside trials were awarded to Marconi, and the Tower Bridge contract was awarded to Chubb. A series of meetings were then held at each of the participating courts with the service suppliers, where lines of communication were set up and duties were specified. In addition, various other matters had to be formalised such as the location of the service suppliers and the equipment, where the fitting of the bracelet and induction would take place, vetting checks on the suppliers' staff by police, the kind of ID cards to be used by the staff, car parking space, etc. A formal liaison committee, chaired by the Home Office, was set up at each of the three sites for the duration of the trials.

It should be evident from the foregoing account that preparation for the electronic monitoring trials was a time-consuming and complicated process; as soon as one problem seemed to be resolved another one appeared, and procedures were continuously being refined and altered to suit changing circumstances. Two points should be emphasised in all of this: first, that such alterations in proposed operating procedures were to be expected given the novel nature of electronic monitoring; and second, that all of these alterations were going on in a vacuum *before* the trials had begun. Such factors had an important impact upon the research.

The research and its methodological difficulties

As soon as a decision had been taken to carry out what was referred to as an 'experiment' (and the term is a significant one) with electronic monitoring, it became logically necessary to require an evaluation of the success or failure of the experiment. The task of carrying out research to supply material for this evaluation fell to the Research and Planning Unit of the Home Office (with some assistance from Statistical Department), while a technical evaluation of the equipment used was carried out by the Scientific Research and Development Branch (SRDB). It was agreed immediately that the evaluation should aim to provide answers to four questions:[(1)]

i. Is electronic monitoring being used as an alternative to a remand in custody?

ii. How successful is monitoring as a condition of bail?

iii. What are the practical issues involved in the use of electronic monitoring?

iv. How cost-effective is monitoring compared to other conditions of bail and to remands in custody?

The researchers were involved in the trials from the beginning. They were members of the Steering Group set up in the Home Office to oversee the progress of the initiative, and also sat on the local liaison committees for each area. Data collection procedures were set up, observation of the schemes and discussions and interviews with those participating were carried out. In normal criminological research terms all of this may sound non-contentious, but there were special difficulties for the research which made it much more complicated and problematic. It is necessary to be clear about these.

The experimental status of electronic monitoring is, perhaps, the most important factor to consider, and it is vital to emphasise that the initiative did not constitute an experiment in any 'scientific' sense. In purely research terms, either of two possible approaches would have been preferred:

i. A decision having been made to try out electronic monitoring and areas chosen, all the agencies involved had simply been allowed scope to develop the practical application of the initiative on their own;

[(1)]The objectives of the research are not the same as those of the trials (p. 2), but they are aimed at helping to inform an assessment of how far the latter have been achieved. Specifically, research objectives i. and ii. relate to trial objective i.; research objective iii. is related to trial objectives i., ii., and iv.; and research objective iv. relates to trial objective iii.

or

ii. the Home Office had controlled every aspect of the trials from beginning to end, and every agency involved had been issued with strict instructions on what should be done at each stage of the monitoring process.

Either of these two approaches would, of course, shape the kind of research which might be carried out—and each would have its own specific methodological weaknesses. The approach which was followed, however, falls somewhere between these two models. Trial areas were informed of the aims and objectives of electronic monitoring and were issued with general guidelines and instructions, but they were also given some discretion in the application and interpretation of these guidelines (and, of course, areas communicated with each other about their practices). Complicating the matter further, the exercise of such discretion had to be reported to the Home Office administrator overseeing the trials and agreed with him.

It is understandable from a Home Office administrative perspective why such an approach should be followed; given the controversial nature of electronic monitoring it would have been unacceptable to give agencies a free hand to develop practice without any central guidance; and it would have been exceptionally difficult to attempt to control every step of the initiative. From a research perspective, however, the approach taken raised serious methodological problems.

Built irreversibly into this approach is the possibility of procedural change without the control or knowledge of the researchers. As has been noted in the previous chapter, a set of procedures had to be organised for the police, CPS and court officials as well as the service suppliers prior to the introduction of monitoring. It should come as no surprise that as soon as the trials had begun, and for much of their duration, procedural changes had to be made. This is not so much a reflection of the fact that the planned procedures were proving to be a failure—although this was the case in some situations. It is much more to do with the fact that there is a considerable gap between devising procedures in theory and putting them into practice; new eventualities occurred, organisational and operational obstacles which hampered the flow of information appeared, and people simply forgot some of the instructions which they had been given. To make matters even more complicated, new players were brought into the game after it had begun; and the various forms designed to be used in the trials were revised on several occasions. Trying to keep fully informed of all these changes proved to be an impossible task for the researchers.

Another factor which had implications for the research, and which was closely related to the issue of procedural change, was the understandable desire to maximise the opportunities for the trials to be successful. As a test project, if no defendants had been considered eligible for electronic monitoring this would not have meant that the trials had failed. On the other hand, however, such an outcome would have meant that all of the objectives of the trials (see p. 2) could not have been adequately met. Thus efforts were made to ensure that enough defendants were monitored to make sense of the initiative. Ultimately, this involved encouraging the police and the CPS to make recommendations for monitoring within the agreed guidelines, and also—with their agreement—to make changes to procedures which might stimulate more recommendations. In Nottingham this led to efforts being made to secure the co-operation of voluntary hostels (ie those not run by the probation service) in providing accommodation as there was a feeling that lack of suitable accommodation was hindering recommendations for monitoring; the police agreed to reconsider their interpretation of the criteria for recommending electronic monitoring; and all agencies were encouraged to examine their practices with regard to recommendations during meetings of the local liaison committee. In the final instance, of course, if the courts had not used electronic monitoring as a condition of bail the number of recommendations made would not have mattered.

It should be emphasised again that these complicating factors for the research arise from the nature of the trials; it is not that they were 'wrong' in any way, or that they demonstrate failures in conception or organisation. Any new project, particularly one such as this where inter-agency co-operation was necessary, is likely to have teething problems which require resolution. The structural aspects of the initiative were set from the start, but local parameters had to be changed and redefined for good administrative reasons. If an action research project had been possible the difficulties posed by these issues might have been minimised, but this would have needed a very different set of circumstances.

As the planning of the trials continued it became increasingly clear that it would be very difficult to draw any firm conclusions from them, partly because of their exploratory nature which meant that procedures were untested; and partly because, when the trials were underway, it quickly became apparent that relatively few defendants were being considered and accepted for electronic monitoring. In addition, the trials were only projected to run for six months (although the possibility of extension for a further six month period was left open)—not really long enough to allow the system to settle down—and the arrangements were slightly different in each of the three areas. Thus the focus of the research changed to concentrate more upon providing an account of the trials (see question iii, p. 14), although the other three objectives will be commented upon as far as possible.

4 The trials

In this chapter an account will be given of the progress of the electronic monitoring initiative in each of the three trial sites during the six months of the trial. The practices and views of representatives of each of the criminal justice agencies involved will be described in order to help assess how far the trials succeeded as an operational accomplishment (the views of those monitored will be discussed in Chapter 6). The researchers attended meetings of the local liaison committees, spent some time observing those involved in the monitoring process at work and discussed electronic monitoring with them; in addition, a few rather more formal, semi-structured interviews were carried out with magistrates and judges.

Nottingham

Prior to the beginning of the trial in each area, the service providers were required to undergo stringent tests in order to satisfy the Home Office that the hardware, software and level of service to be provided came up to the necessary standards. In the event, three acceptance tests were necessary for the Nottingham trial: Marconi failed the first because the equipment would not function over the British Telecom network and the staff recruited had not been trained to a sufficiently high standard; and they failed the second as the required standard had still not been reached with the staff who would be working on the project on the ground. The third test was satisfactory, but the two failures only added to the general level of apprehension and nervousness which surrounded the opening of the first trial (indeed, there was some doubt at one stage of the acceptance tests whether the trial would begin on the planned date). As a result of these problems, Marconi were obliged to provide and train a replacement team of operators which would run in parallel with the existing team. If the latter's performance did not reach the required standard, the new team would be deployed. The management team for the project agreed to monitor the performance of the operators closely during the first few weeks of the trial.

The Nottingham trial began on 14 August with a good deal of media interest and the police, CPS, and court clerks all prepared to play their parts. Unfortunately, this all proved to be somewhat of an anti-climax as no-one was monitored on the first day or the second. There were, however, several recommendations for electronic monitoring from the police and defence solicitors; and one of these (from the police) almost succeeded. The defendant in question fitted all the relevant criteria, but lived in landlady accommodation. When the landlady was approached for her agreement to the installation of the monitoring equipment she refused because she claimed that she could not deal with all the publicity which would ensue following the first person to be monitored.

On the third day the first order for electronic monitoring was made, although as a phone had to be installed monitoring did not begin until the following day (17 August 1989). Richard Hart was charged with nine offences and had been remanded in custody; the recommendation for electronic monitoring as a condition of bail was made by his defence solicitor. Hart was 23 years old, married and his wife had just had a baby (his defence solicitor claimed that the recommendation was *not* based upon this fact); his curfew was set at 21 hours and his permitted hours of absence were from 9.00 a.m. to 12.00 noon each day. The induction procedure whereby the equipment and how it worked were explained to Hart was carried out well by the service suppliers, as was the fitting of the bracelet to the defendant's ankle—which took place under television cameras.

On the same day as Hart was accepted another three defendants were assessed by the police as possible candidates for monitoring; one of these was refused by the CPS, one was not put forward because his mother stated that she could not cope with him at home because of his psychiatric/drink problems, and the third seemed to be a good case. The defendant in this case talked the matter over with his solicitor and refused to be considered for monitoring; during a brief interview later, he stated that he was worried about the publicity which would be involved if he was to be the first person monitored, and he was clearly unsure how the system worked as he thought his home would be 'bugged'. He was granted bail with a condition of residence at a bail hostel.

As might have been expected, a series of logistical and operational matters which had not been anticipated had to be resolved. In cases where defence solicitors recommended electronic monitoring but the court rejected this, no data collection forms were being completed. The details of who would be responsible for such forms in Crown Court cases needed clarification. The flow of forms after CPS involvement was not very clear. And various amendments to the forms were needed. There was also a question about who would be responsible for removing the transmitter-bracelet for those who were in custody, and those in Crown Court. And the matter of consent needed to be looked at: defence solicitors might be too keen to put forward their clients for monitoring when they had not discussed it with them and they were in custody.

One very positive development involved the police initiating a central filtering system for all recommendations for monitoring which originated from their officers. This involved each new case and all re-remand cases being checked by a Chief Inspector and a Detective Inspector each morning for their eligibility for monitoring. This process was initiated to try to ensure that no potential candidate slipped through the net, and it also brought a degree of consistency to police decisions (there were eight police stations feeding into this process). At the start of the trials, the Chief Inspector was spending about 10 hours each day in the cell block to try to ensure smooth running of the system (although his direct participation diminished over time).

A meeting of the local liaison committee was held 10 days after the start of the trial, by which time there had been about a dozen recommendations but only one success. There were signs of frustration, particularly on the part of the police, that so few were being monitored and the question which dominated the proceedings was why this was the case. No simple answer emerged, but several useful points were made which appeared to have a bearing upon this issue. The police questioned their role in the decision-making process for monitoring; it was difficult to go back over decisions which had already been made to try to identify those who, but for electronic monitoring, should be remanded in custody (there may also have been a feeling that having worked hard to identify potential participants they were disappointed that none of their recommendations had been accepted). There was a view—though no real evidence to substantiate it—that one reason for the low numbers lay in the lack of suitable accommodation for some potential candidates; some interest had been expressed in providing accommodation by a housing trust and this was to be followed up. The opposition of defence solicitors, lack of time for consideration by CPS, the magistrates being cautious, the fact that it was still early days for the trial, and the police had always said that there would be few potential candidates—all of these were mentioned as lying behind the low numbers.

On the weekend before the liaison committee meeting, there had been a violation alarm of 3.5 hours (a level 2 violation) for Richard Hart. All the planned procedures seemed to have been followed correctly by the operators although there was uncertainty about whether the alarm was due to equipment problems or Hart's absence (he claimed that he had been present all night). There was some embarrassment, however, on the part of the court and the Home Office that this first alleged violation was brought to their attention by the press; it was arranged that in future, both the justices' clerk and the Home Office should be informed by the service suppliers of any level 2 violation.

As the weeks went past a series of relatively minor problems and issues continued to appear in the procedures which had been set up. None of these led to any major changes in the system, but they did mean that any formal evaluation of a set procedure would be impossible. Only the more important changes in procedures will be considered in what follows. Details of the data collection forms were amended fairly often, but perhaps the most significant change was that 'valid' applications for monitoring by defence solicitors were to be collected. The issue here, of course, was what exactly was meant by 'valid'—and this question was not completely resolved; it was decided that a 'valid' application would be one which the defence solicitor made from the start of his argument, and would not apply where a suggestion for monitoring was thrown in at the last minute as a final effort. Clearly, a grey area remained here.

As a result of the feeling that lack of accommodation was a barrier to potential participants, the police agreed to mark the data collection forms in appropriate instances as 'recommended for EM subject to provision of suitable accommodation' (in the event, only two forms were so marked). A hostel run by a housing trust was made available for candidates for monitoring who needed accommodation, but there was no evidence that this improved the flow of defendants who were recommended or monitored. Indeed, the use of the hostel raised interesting questions about the length of the curfew period and the need for some form of social work support for those who were monitored there. The first two defendants who were monitored in the hostel had curfews of 23 and 24 hours. The defendant with the 24 hour curfew absconded a few days after monitoring began, but gave himself up to the police the next day. He left a message on the wall of his room stating "You treat tagged people with no respect. You are choosing me for an example". Hostel staff considered that there were several contributory factors behind this violation: the length of the curfew involved, the date of the defendant's trial being postponed at short notice, and a relationship which had not worked out.

The hostel staff were keen to help as far as possible to try to keep people out of custody, and this was why they had decided to become involved in the trial. There were some initial difficulties about the location of telephones and the role of hostel staff in relation to alleged violations, but these were clarified. Hostel staff thought that monitoring might be useful if used sparingly, but was not perhaps such a good idea in a hostel setting and particularly if long curfew hours were used. They also stressed that there was a need for some kind of counselling for those being monitored, and that the probation service could play a vital part in this. They were also apprehensive about the possibility of net-widening, whereby those being monitored would, in its absence, have received bail with other conditions and not have been remanded in custody.

By the end of October 12 defendants had been monitored in Nottingham, five of whom had appeared at the Crown Court. As a result of the Crown Court use, detailed procedures had to be organised for the personnel involved and the acceptance form agreeing to electronic monitoring had to be redrafted. Neither Crown Court staff nor the police were prepared to remove the transmitter-bracelet from a defendant when he/she was acquitted or received a non-custodial sentence at the Crown Court; the service operators were expected to be aware of this possibility and to arrange for the retrieval of any equipment.

Efforts continued to be made during the course of the trial to increase the numbers being recommended for monitoring and actually being monitored. The police were asked to reconsider their approach to the guidelines which had been set up prior to the trial and did so, but this had no discernible effect. On the one hand, the police were keen to help and far more recommendations were made by them than in either of the other two areas (see Table 2, Chapter 5); but they were also very aware of the need to consider public safety, and were perhaps rather frustrated that so few of their recommendations were accepted by the CPS.

Early in November, while 'fine-tuning' of procedures continued, the various options for ending the trial had to be discussed. The original plan had been for a six-month trial with the possibility of extension on a monthly basis. Four options were identified: ending the trial on 29 January; continuing the trial with or without a new end-date; running a monitoring only service after 29 January until all cases had been disposed of by the courts; or running a monitoring only service after 29 January but with a set end-date. These options were discussed by the liaison committee which decided to recommend that the intake of new defendants would cease at midnight on 29 January, and that a monitoring only service would continue until 30 April or before if the last case was disposed of by the courts before then. It was hoped that this approach would not lead to any reduction in the number of recommendations or acceptances for electronic monitoring. In fact, the number of defendants being monitored had been declining before the mid-point of the trial was reached (see Chart 2, Chapter 5). The recommendation for ending the trial was accepted by the Home Office and electronic monitoring ceased to be available in Nottingham after 29 January 1990.

In all, there were 68 recommendations for electronic monitoring in Nottingham; 62 of these occurred in the magistrates' court and six in the Crown Court. A total of 17 defendants were monitored, 11 from the magistrates' court and six (ie all who were recommended) in the Crown Court. The bulk of recommendations originated from defence solicitors (51), while 14 were made by the police, one by the CPS and two by magistrates. The success rate of these recommendations is set out in Table 2, Chapter 5.

The introduction of electronic monitoring necessitated some alterations in the normal practices of the criminal justice agencies involved, and also required new forms of co-ordination and liaison. In concluding this account of the Nottingham trial, the performance of each of the agencies will be discussed.

The police

The police in Nottingham were particularly keen to help with the trial and interested in its progress; one measure of this lies in the fact that of the 15 recommendations made in total by the police during the course of the three trials, 14 of these were made by the Nottingham police. From the beginning of the plans for the trial, however, they had been insistent that there was little scope for electronic monitoring in the area as potential participants would be thin on the ground; a curfew as a condition of bail was already used in Nottingham, and the introduction of electronic monitoring to this was not seen as providing any real advantages. Despite their pessimism as to possible numbers, a central filtering system was set up to check on all recommendations; in terms of the trial, this seems to have been a helpful initiative—the CPS certainly thought so—although whether it could be sustained over a long period is uncertain (indeed, some police officers made independent recommendations for monitoring as an alternative to bail with a curfew, although the CPS agreed to reject these).

It should be noted that the police were uneasy about their involvement in recommending defendants for monitoring, a decision which was not considered to be part of normal police work. Having said this, however, it should be added that they were not satisfied with the low numbers of defendants monitored and showed themselves to be willing to reconsider their interpretation of the guidelines for selection of potential candidates; it was the police who brought up the question of lack of suitable accommodation. The police also kept a close watch on the number of alleged violations by those monitored, and on several occasions spoke to defence solicitors about the number of level 1 violations by their clients; interestingly enough, this seemed to result in a drop in the number of such violations. One worry for the police resulted from the lack of information about cases where the defendant had been charged with offences which were alleged to have taken place outside the petty sessional division, but these had been transferred to the Nottingham magistrates' court. The police adhered to the guidelines which stated that only those who had allegedly committed offences within the jurisdiction of the PSD should be considered for electronic monitoring. All of this police activity had resource implications, and these were commented upon by senior police officers on several occasions.

The Chief Inspector responsible for liaison was, in the end, reasonably satisfied with the police role in the trial. He had been particularly concerned about the demands on police resources at the beginning, but these had not turned out to be too problematic because the numbers had been so low. He felt that the time taken for a remand hearing had been slowed down considerably whenever the possibility of electronic monitoring was being considered; the time had come down as clerks, magistrates, CPS and defence solicitors had become accustomed to the process, but it was still much longer than before the trial had started. He was not wholly convinced of the efficacy of the equipment—defendants always blamed the equipment in the event of an alleged violation, and it was vital to be certain whether or not this was the case. And he also raised the issue of how one could be sure that it was the defendant who answered the telephone when a violation check was being done. He was clear that those monitored needed extra support and that input from the probation service would be an appropriate way of providing this.

The CPS

The CPS only generated one recommendation independently of the police for electronic monitoring—and this failed—but while taking a less active role than the police they remained interested. The remand courts were very busy and it was suggested that the prosecutors did not have enough time to make considered decisions on potential candidates for monitoring. On the other hand, however, they did advise the bench in cases where defence solicitors made what were viewed as inappropriate applications for monitoring. CPS representatives also noted the size of the Nottingham bench—more than 500 lay magistrates—which they felt was a disadvantage for the trial; it would be very difficult to get across to so many the aims of the trial, and the criteria to be used in selecting participants. Defence solicitors presented a similar problem.

The senior Crown Prosecutor who acted as liaison for the trial thought that the magistrates found it difficult to identify defendants who might be monitored; he saw a tendency whereby when an appropriate person was identified, there then came a view that bail with a curfew might be just as effective. This fitted in with a phenomenon which was noted in the first week of the trial; when a good case was put up for monitoring by the defence solicitor the defendant was bailed with conditions. This would suggest that simply the presence of electronic monitoring could, in some cases, lead to the granting of bail where a remand in custody might otherwise have resulted.

The CPS also felt that there was too much paperwork involved in the initiative, and that no consistent pattern of use of monitoring had emerged from the Crown Court. They were aware of their low recommendation rate, but argued that potential participants would be spotted by the police before they reached CPS. Suggestions made for future developments included restricting monitoring to those who had breached a curfew, restricting its use to the Crown Court, and lowering the age-range to 16.

The courts

The main point about the magistrates' court in Nottingham was its size, as has already been noted. Trying to ensure that all magistrates were fully aware of the availability of electronic monitoring and the guidelines for using it was always likely to be a very difficult task, especially within six months. The court clerks were seen to be crucial in this situation and a good deal of effort was spent in acquainting them with the requirements of electronic monitoring. They, in turn, tried to communicate with the magistrates in a variety of ways including training sessions, a bench circular, and information in the retiring room. The clerks also tried to address the issue of monitoring only being used as an alternative to a remand in custody, but it should be noted that their role is a strictly advisory one.

The clerks were wary at the start because of the publicity involved in being the first court in the country to have electronic monitoring available, because of what they saw as the complexity of the legal issues involved, and the amount of paperwork which was needed. In practice, and as a consequence of the low numbers, the resource implications had not been as bad as expected. Court hearings when monitoring was considered were agreed to have taken longer than normal, as a clerk always advised the bench in such cases and solicitors tended to have to present arguments carefully. The increase in the length of time, however, demonstrated that magistrates were considering carefully cases where monitoring had been recommended, and this also helped to avoid net-widening which had been a potential unintended consequence of the trial but which was considered to have been successfully overcome.

Electronic monitoring was seen by the clerks as having some application in sentencing, though they were by no means certain of its usefulness as an alternative to a remand in custody. The possible advantages of monitoring had not been brought out by the trial, particularly the degree of flexibility which could be offered. The need for probation involvement in explaining electronic monitoring to defendants before any application was made, as well as providing counselling and support for those monitored was again emphasised.

Brief interviews were carried out with three magistrates, one of whom was the Chairman of the Bench. One of the three had sat on a bench where monitoring had been used contrary to her advice (the defendant absconded), while the other two had not found anyone suitable. None of them considered that electronic monitoring had made any real impact upon the bail/remand decision, although they felt that they had been given enough information about the system to use it confidently; in this respect, they mentioned the amount of training and presentations given by the court clerks. Each of them commented on the difficulties in finding suitable candidates for monitoring, and one noted that having decided that a defendant should be remanded in custody it was very difficult to go back on that and consider monitoring. Two of the three saw no clear advantages or disadvantages in electronic monitoring (the low numbers were a factor here), while the third thought it was an ideal approach in theory but choosing suitable participants was not easy. Monitoring was not seen to provide a practicable alternative to a remand in custody. All agreed that it was difficult to assess the suitability of someone for monitoring in the short time available; a relatively stable background with a job, home and family were mentioned by one, while another felt that it was an attitude of mind which was needed. The possible role of the probation service in this area was noted. Finally, while all three felt that the trial had succeeded in identifying many teething problems with monitoring, they were unconvinced that electronic monitoring had any part to play in the criminal justice system.

Although detailed planning was not made for Crown Court participation in advance of the trial, the Nottingham Crown Court contributed significantly to the use of electronic monitoring; more than one-third of those monitored came form the Crown Court (six out of seventeen), and out of eight in total from the Crown Courts in all three trial sites, six came from Nottingham. The two judges who used electronic monitoring were interviewed jointly. One of them felt that monitoring had made a difference to his decision-making with regard to bail/remand, while the other thought it had made no difference at all. They were unhappy that they had not been consulted prior to the trial, and expressed the hope that in the event of any future initiatives there would be full consultation with judges. The advantage of monitoring was that it had worked for some defendants, but its disadvantage was that most participants had either absconded or had been arrested for a further offence. Both agreed that electronic monitoring could provide a practicable alternative to a custodial remand, especially if a tamper-proof bracelet was used (this was not used in the Nottingham trial) and curfews of around 23 hours were made—although if the defendant had a job this could be reduced. Monitoring should not be used for those charged with the most serious offences, or if there was a long history of breaches of bail; a settled home and community ties were needed, although lack of knowledge about the defendant was noted as a key problem, particularly when he/she was not present in person for the application. Both judges considered that monitoring had a place in the criminal justice system, but not as an alternative to remand; too few people were eligible in this area to make it financially viable. They saw it as a sentence of the court which might be used as an alternative to a custodial sentence and in conjuction with a community service order or a fine. The value of the trial as an experiment was endorsed by both respondents.

The service providers

Despite the apprehensions caused by the problems encountered by the acceptance tests, and some initial failures to follow specified procedures, the service operators seem to have performed well. The replacement team was stood down after three weeks. All the other agencies were satisfied with the way the operators had carried out their tasks. The induction procedure and the attachment of the bracelet to a defendant's ankle were carried out smoothly and explained clearly. Response to violations kept closely to the agreed guidelines, though by the end of the trial violations of only a minute or two tended to be ignored. The operators noticed quickly that most of those monitored seemed to test out the system fairly soon after monitoring began; they would be a few minutes late at the beginning of their curfew, or a few minutes early in leaving at the end of it. The operators themselves enjoyed the job, though they considered the paperwork to be excessive (this was partly a result of the police/CPS insistence that a witness statement should be completed for every alleged violation). They were bored at times when there was little to do and were rather disappointed that so few people had been monitored. They felt that the inter-personal aspect of the work was very important and that training should concentrate more on this. They were at times surprised at how co-operative some defendants could be; one defendant, on a 24 hour curfew except on Mondays when he did community service, arranged a visit to the dentist a week in advance, informed the operators and gave them the dentist's phone number; he later phoned to ask if he could go out on a Monday when his community service was not going on. They also noted what they termed 'informed violations' when a police informer was monitored and the CID would ring in to say that the defendant was going out with them.

During the 24 weeks of the trial and the two weeks after it when defendants who were being monitored were dealt with in court, there were 22 equipment failures recorded:

7	– internal fuse on Home Unit
4	– other Home Unit failure
4	– 0800 line failures
2	– possible deadspots
2	– uninterrupted power supply failure
1	– BT line fault (other than 0800)
1	– number pad on telephone sticking (defendant's own phone)
1	– transmitter lost
22	

Others involved

Various other organisations were involved in the trial in a more peripheral role. They had little direct involvement and were not included in any of the planning, but their attitudes and practices could be relevant for the successful implementation of electronic monitoring. The local probation service was not part of the trial and its stance towards monitoring was negative, but a representative from the service was invited to sit on the liaison committee and did so. It has already been shown that many of those involved in the trial considered that there was a need for the involvement of the probation service, and this was accepted by the service representative.

The use of the hostel has been discussed, but it should be emphasised that the workers did not really see a hostel as an ideal environment for someone being monitored; they had agreed to get involved to try to keep people out of custody.

In planning the trial it was recognised that defence solicitors could play an important role in generating candidates for monitoring, but there was no simple and effective method of communicating to all of them the aims of the trial and the guidelines to be followed (although a Home Office official did address the local Law Society on this topic). In the event, defence solicitors proved to be by far the most common source for recommendations for electronic monitoring (51 out of 68 in all came from this source, 45 in the magistrates' court and six in Crown Court). Despite this, members of the liaison committee considered that defence solicitors were not following guidelines consistently, for example they made 'last-ditch' applications which were not well presented, and on occasion their clients were not informed that they were to be recommended for monitoring. It is unfortunate that a decision was taken not to collect information on all applications from defence solicitors (only 'valid' applications were collected, see above), as such material might have demonstrated how far defence solicitors strayed from the criteria. It was suggested that defence solicitors began to lose interest in the trial soon after the half-way stage, and that in fact only one firm of solicitors had been keen and had generated the bulk of applications. Both of these points may show that this group was not fully aware of the nature of the trial.

The Prison Officers' Association (POA) wrote to the Home Office objecting to any prison service dock officer involvement in the monitoring trial, but this did not lead to any serious problems. Apart from this, the role of the prison service in the trial was to hold overnight defendants who had been granted bail with a condition of electronic monitoring but did not have a telephone. In Nottingham, wherever possible the police kept such cases in holding cells, but when this could not be done the defendant had to be taken to Lincoln prison and then taken back the next day. Logistically and financially this was not a particularly efficient process.

There were no problems with British Telecom in the installation of equipment.

Finally, where a defendant had an extensive curfew the local Department of Social Security initially considered that he could be regarded as not being available for work and his benefit cut accordingly. Efforts were made to assure DSS that curfews could be varied (and no further specific problems came to light), but it is difficult to know whether anxiety about the possibility of benefit cuts had any impact upon the generation of candidates for electronic monitoring.

North Tyneside

Once again the first acceptance test for the service provider—Marconi—was failed due to the unreliability of the tamper-alert mechanism (which had not been used in Nottingham) on the transmitter-bracelet. The second test was passed after some further work had been done on the appropriate mechanism.

The trial at North Tyneside began on 18 September, five weeks after Nottingham had commenced and it was hoped that some of the early difficulties in Nottingham would be avoided as a result of lessons which had been learnt. Prior to the start of the trial, training and demonstrations for the various staff had been carried out and some of the agencies involved had been in contact with their counterparts in Nottingham. It was possible to plan in rather more detail the procedure to be followed in the Crown Court when a defendant was to be monitored; prison officers (in their capacity as dock officers) agreed to telephone the service operators to alert them to this. The service operators were located in the police station (in Nottingham they were based in the court), and it was agreed that defendants awaiting the installation of equipment would be held in police custody. Only three police stations fed into the court which was considerably smaller than Nottingham (there were around 90 lay magistrates); overall, the much smaller numbers involved in this trial suggested that communication and liaison would be a simpler matter than at Nottingham.

By the fifth day of the trial no successful applications for electronic monitoring had been made, and reasons for this were being sought. One factor was that the number of overnight arrests had dropped by about one-third during the first week of the trial, though no-one could offer any explanation for this. It was also suggested that many potential participants were of no fixed abode as the area had recently lost the use of a voluntary hostel. One slightly worrying development had been that the bench had refused to consider that the availability of electronic monitoring constituted a change of circumstances in re-remand cases where monitoring had been recommended by defence solicitors. It seemed, however, that each case was dealt with on an individual basis, and while monitoring might not be seen to amount to a change in circumstances for some, that did not mean that it would be seen in this way for all.

There seemed to be a good deal of uncertainty and lack of organising for the trial in North Tyneside. There was no central filtering system set up by the police, and no meeting between the interested parties every morning as took place in Nottingham. It became clear that the police would not, in fact, be able to hold overnight those who had been approved for monitoring but awaited equipment installation. While people were helpful there was a distinct lack of interest and motivation; nobody seemed to want to grasp the nettle of electronic monitoring, to take the lead in the initiative, although the court staff were doing their best to keep things going. Indeed, it was the clerk with liaison responsibility for the trial who suggested that the police, the CPS and himself should meet each morning in an effort to stimulate recommendations for monitoring. This was agreed, but only on the basis of a two-week trial which would assess how useful the meetings were.

By 29 October, six weeks into the trial, 16 recommendations had been made—all of them by defence solicitors—and six defendants had been monitored. By this time it was clear that there was little effective co-ordination between the various agencies, and several other problems had appeared.

In the first place, it became evident that North Tyneside should not perhaps have been chosen for the trial. One of the factors in choosing an area had been the number of remands and North Tyneside had appeared to fulfil this criterion; unfortunately, this high remand rate was a 'false' one as the court had a tendency to remand defendants in custody for a week in order that bail information could be gathered about them, and then grant bail with conditions (an 'informal' bail information scheme was found to exist in the area). This meant that there were fewer potential candidates for electronic monitoring than had been envisaged originally.

The tripartite meetings had taken place for two weeks but no recommendations had emerged. The meetings had not continued, partly because they had not helped to generate recommendations, although it was also suggested that lack of interest by the police had played a part. The police view was that the meetings had been held to make sure that the guideline criteria for potential candidates were being adhered to, and that when this had been ensured there was no need to carry on with them.

A gap in the liaison system had emerged with the first four defendants to be monitored (all were part of the same case). The defendants had been recommended by defence solicitors and accepted by the bench at 4.50 on a Friday afternoon. The court clerk telephoned the operators to say that the defendants were being sent to the police station, but it had been made clear by the police that they were not prepared to hold such defendants overnight (the plan had been to make sure that anyone to be monitored should be accepted by lunchtime, and that defendants would have to be returned to the remand centre if they could not be put on the system that day). The police had found out about these first candidates for monitoring from the press, and felt that the court clerks should have informed them. Matters were made worse when the same thing happened several days later.

At the same time there had been a series of problems with the equipment, all of them resulting from the tamper-alert mechanism. The service operators had been going out once or twice a day to check when tamper-alert mechanisms had been activated, but these had all been false positives. Now, instead of wasting time they simply telephoned the defendant when this happened to check that he was still at his residence. All violations of curfews—even those lasting only for a minute or two—were reported to the police. Many of these were found to be programming faults, but had been recorded as violations on the defendant's record and would be produced at court.

A problem also arose with a defendant who was being monitored and who went back to court asking for a change in his curfew hours because he had found a job; the court refused. Court clerks were asked to ensure that magistrates were aware that it was open to them to change curfews in such circumstances. There were difficulties in transporting defendants back from prison or remand centre in order to be fitted with the bracelet. And the service providers felt that British Telecom were not keeping in close enough contact with them; on several occasions they had been to residences to install equipment some hours before they had said they would, which meant that defendants could have been put on the system earlier.

In an effort to stimulate recommendations for monitoring the police designed a form which listed the criteria for selection of candidates; when these applied to a defendant he/she would be recommended for monitoring, when they did not reasons would be stated. This form was then passed to the CPS. Unfortunately it was not possible to arrange access to these forms for the researchers.

By mid-December 12 defendants had been monitored. Members of the liaison committee considered that appropriate cases were simply not coming up; there was a lack of suitable candidates for monitoring in the area. The police were uneasy about alleged violations which were claimed to have been caused when defendants were in the bath. The service providers pointed out that water did reduce the intensity of the signals sent from the bracelet, but not to the extent of a violation being recorded; this explanation of 'being in the bath' had been given persistently by one defendant. It was agreed that the best way to deal with this was for the operators to visit the defendant's home the next time this happened, test the equipment in a filled bath and demonstrate that the signals were still relayed to the Home Unit. The police were keen that this information should be disseminated as widely as possible in order to deter others from using the same excuse, and suggested that they and the service operators should try to ensure that the results of the 'bath test' were reported in a local newspaper.

The first example of a defendant tampering with equipment in order to get round the system occurred in January. He had been going out outside his curfew hours and claiming that there was a fault on his telephone line. British Telecom had been to check three times before they noticed the cause; the defendant had been fiddling with the wires in the telephone. This was a useful episode for the operators for they now felt that they had knowledge of a loophole which they could check themselves in the future. It was also noted that several defendants refused to be monitored, presumably because, unlike a remand in custody, time on monitoring would not count against the custodial sentence.

The North Tyneside trial ended on 5 March, with the same run-down procedure as in Nottingham (three months during which those already on the system would be monitored and arrangements would be made to try to have their cases dealt with in that time). Very few new participants were accepted for monitoring in the second half of the trial; only three and one of these was from the Crown Court.

A total of 35 recommendations for electronic monitoring had been made during the trial; 26 of these had been made in the magistrates' court and nine in the Crown Court. 15 defendants were monitored, all but one in the magistrates' court. Thirty-one of the recommendations came from defence solicitors, two from magistrates, one from a judge, and one from the police. While the low involvement in recommendations of the CPS and magistrates parallels the situation in Nottingham, North Tyneside differed in that the police only managed one recommendation for electronic monitoring.

The role of each of the agencies will now be considered briefly.

The police

The police in North Tyneside were helpful and not in any way hostile towards the trial, but there was little motivation and no signs of actively encouraging the trial. This lack of interest percolated down to the lower ranks where there seemed to be a clear lack of knowledge about electronic monitoring and the aims and objectives of the trial. The service operators spoke of police calling in to see them in order to find out what was going on. As has been noted, there was no centralised decision-making process with regard to bail/remand, and although they were aware of the filtering system set up by the Nottingham police for the trial there was no attempt to replicate this in North Tyneside.

Police relationships with the other agencies involved in the trial varied. They seemed to get on well with the service operators, and police officers would drop in for a chat or to discuss cases; they enquired about curfew hours on defendants, and on at least one occasion mentioned to an operator that a defendant had been seen in town (he had been outside his curfew hours at the time). This relationship was informal and not based upon official liaison system; it was obviously based upon the fact that the service operators were located in the police HQ (unlike Nottingham, where they were based in the magistrates' court buildings). But liaison with the CPS was not particularly efficient; the police claimed that any recommendations were sent out to the CPS HQ in the morning, but a court clerk stated that prosecutors did not see defendants' papers until just before they got into court. Communication between the police and court clerks was poor.

A major police concern (and this had also been apparent in Nottingham) was their responsibility for public safety. This was mentioned by the police on several occasions as one reason for the lack of recommendations for monitoring; given that they see themselves as policing to ensure public safety, it is perhaps not surprising that they tend to be very cautious about recommending bail—even when it is subject to electronic monitoring—in the case of a defendant for whom they would normally oppose bail. For one defendant who had been recommended for monitoring by his solicitor, the police put forward a four-page report arguing that he was not suitable as they considered him to be too much of a danger to the public.

The police officer who was responsible for liaison during the trial felt that there was a role for the police in any such initiative, despite the lack of recommendations from them. She considered that the trial had demonstrated that the equipment functioned, although the numbers monitored had been low; ultimately, she felt that the remand cases in court simply did not fall within the guidelines specified. The trial had been a useful experience which could be built upon. She thought that monitoring should not be used as an alternative to a remand in custody, but would be useful in monitoring curfews.

The CPS

In general, the CPS in North Tyneside had a much lower profile in the trial than was the case in Nottingham. Although they made no recommendations for electronic monitoring they seemed to be fully aware of the criteria to be considered and willing to apply these whenever possible. The CPS view, however, was that there simply were not enough appropriate cases in the area to generate an adequate number of cases for monitoring. The CPS rarely disagreed with police recommendations about bail/remand as they considered that the police had much greater detailed knowledge of specific cases. While CPS–Court liaison was good, there did appear to be something of a problem in CPS–police communication which may not have helped the trial. The prosecutors were helpful in informing the service operators whenever a monitored defendant was appearing in court and when the court appearance was over.

Prosecutors did not feel that accommodation was causing problems in potential monitoring cases; they claimed that most NFA (no fixed abode) cases were granted conditional bail (and therefore would not be considered for monitoring), or that accommodation had been found for them by the time they appeared in court. The trial had not caused any particular drain on CPS resources, although the amount of paperwork involved was commented upon. The CPS viewed electronic monitoring as most suitable for older defendants, and that it should only be used for relatively short periods of up to three months.

The courts

There were considerably fewer magistrates in North Tyneside than in Nottingham, and this seemed to make the task of the court clerks in trying to communicate to them the aims of the trial and its guidelines much simpler. The liaison clerk worked hard to keep people informed about electronic monitoring (he also gave a talk on it to local defence solicitors), but despite this there were some breakdowns in liaison between the courts and the police over the first few cases to be monitored. It may be worth noting that the much smaller size of the operation and the more informal nature of communication and liaison which characterised the area may have been a disadvantage to the trial, in that members of the various criminal justice agencies were not perhaps accustomed to the more formal liaison arrangements which were put into place for the trial.

The liaison clerk had little to say about the trial as so few had been monitored. He felt that the equipment had worked, but that monitoring should only be used as another condition of bail rather than as an alternative to a remand in custody. He also noted that cases involving monitoring took considerably longer in court, and that this could lead to serious problems if large numbers were considered for monitoring.

The Justices' Clerk was interviewed towards the end of the trial. He felt that the introduction of electronic monitoring had made less impact than might have been expected; the bench always tried hard not to remand, the criteria had been adhered to closely and few defendants had been elegible. Monitoring was only suitable for those with jobs, and curfews of 20 hours or more were 'a dead loss' as they caused all sorts of domestic problems. Interestingly, he pointed out that defence solicitors were reluctant to recommend monitoring at times if they felt that there was the slightest chance of bail, as such a recommendation might put the idea of a remand in custody into magistrates' heads. He thought that enough information had been given about electronic monitoring, but that it was not a practicable alternative to a custodial remand. If it kept defendants out of custody it would be advantageous, but it was an elaborate and time-consuming process from the magistrates' point of view. There was a place for monitoring, though not as an alternative to a remand in custody; it might be used as part of a sentence or as a condition of bail. But it would have to be used widely to make it economically viable, and probation service involvement would be essential.

The magistrates as a whole were thought to be fairly equally split into three groups in their attitudes to electronic monitoring: one-third in favour, one-third neutral and one-third opposed. Two magistrates were interviewed, one of whom had used electronic monitoring on two occasions while the other had considered it several times but had not used it as the charges had been too serious. Both felt that electronic monitoring had made a little difference to their decision-making insofar as defence solicitors kept bringing it up and therefore it had to be considered, although most of the time it was inappropriate. Neither had been satisfied with the Home Office presentation on monitoring—particularly as colleagues with a knowledge of electronics had pointed out to them how fallible monitoring could be; on the other hand, they thought the advice from court clerks had been very helpful. The respondent who had used monitoring stated that the fact that both defendants had been employed had been a key factor in the decision to use it. And though both had absconded within 24 hours she claimed that this had not changed her attitude towards electronic monitoring. Both respondents saw serious disadvantages in the strain which monitoring could put on families, in the DSS response to participants in terms of their entitlement to benefit, and in the elaborate and lengthy announcement of the details of monitoring which had to be given to participants in court. Monitoring was considered to be suited to those with 'a job, a phone, a wife, a family'. While it was not seen as providing a practicable alternative to a remand in custody, it might be useful as part of a sentence of house arrest (drunk-drivers were mentioned as a possible target-group), though a good deal more piloting was seen as vital before anything was introduced on a permanent basis.

There was little Crown Court involvement in electronic monitoring and no detailed procedures were set up or had time to evolve.

The service providers

Problems with the tamper-alert mechanism (which had resulted in Marconi failing the first acceptance test) continued for the first few months of the trial, but these were eventually resolved and the number of false alarms decreased dramatically after this. The operators performed their tasks efficiently; they explained the system clearly to defendants who were to be monitored and attached the bracelet with a minimum of fuss. The only problem was that operators had to travel to Durham prison or Low Newton remand centre to do this as defendants could not be held overnight by the police.

The criminal justice agencies were satisfied with the performance of the operators—especially the police, as has already been noted. The operators commented on the number of occasions police officers dropped in to discuss the system, and seemed to be impressed that defendants' whereabouts were known (in fact, they would only be known during curfew hours). Boredom and frustration were evident due to the lack of numbers, and one operator mentioned how interesting it had been when five had been monitored at one time.

During the North Tyneside trial (which had run for 28 weeks in all—the original 24 plus four weeks in which monitored cases were dealt with) there were a total of 53 equipment failures, the majority of which were caused by the tamper-alert mechanism.

35	tamper alert mechanism failures
4	transmitter battery failures
3	other Home Unit failures
3	BT line fault (other than 0800)
2	0800 line failure
2	mains power failures (control centre)
1	internal fuse on Home Unit
1	central computer failure
1	transmitter lost
1	transmitter strap broken
53	

Others involved

Northumbria Probation Service was invited to nominate a representative to sit on the liaison committee and did so, though the person nominated was unable to attend any of the meetings. The local probation team was said to be cynical about the trial but not hostile.

The key to the trial was again local defence solicitors who made 31 recommendations for electronic monitoring out of 35. Again, it was not possible before the commencement of the trial to ensure that all defence solicitors were fully aware of the details of monitoring, and—as has been noted—the magistrates' court clerk gave a talk to defence solicitors soon after the trial began. A local solicitor was appointed by the Law Society to keep an eye on developments during the course of the trial; he felt that defence solicitors were very cautious at the start (as were the magistrates). A solicitor whose firm had made several successful recommendations for electronic monitoring was interviewed and he claimed that 95 per cent of solicitors in the area would say it had all been a waste of time. He was especially critical of the length of curfew periods (nine out of fifteen were for between 16 and 23 hours), particularly when used for young people who did not have the necessary self-discipline to cope. Monitoring might have some use for older offenders but shorter curfew periods would be needed, and any time on monitoring should be deducted from sentence.

In practice, prison officers were more helpful than the official attitude of the POA might have led one to believe. Defendants were placed on the system in prison establishments without any problems, but this was time-consuming for the operators and could create difficulties for defendants who had to return to their place of residence within a specified time.

Arrangements with British Telecom (BT) had not gone quite so smoothly as in Nottingham. BT had stated that they could not guarantee to install equipment within 24 hours during weekends; and they would not install equipment after noon on 22 December until the end of the Christmas period (fortunately, there was no need of their services during this period). At one point, it seemed that BT had agreed that a telephone installed at a defendants' home could be removed when monitoring was concluded and redeployed in the home of another defendant who was about to commence monitoring. This would have reduced costs slightly, but BT subsequently stated that this could not be done.

Tower Bridge

Chubb were the service providers for the Tower Bridge trial, but like Marconi in the other two trial areas they failed the first acceptance test prior to the start of the trial. The hardware and software did not meet the contract specifications, the control room procedures were inadequate (in other words, staff had not been properly trained), and there were serious doubts about the quality of project management. These matters were critical enough to raise the possibility of postponing the start of the trial if the Chubb performance did not reach the required standard. In the event, after considerable work by Home Office staff, an acceptable level of operation was reached on the second test and the trial began as planned on 23 October.

As usual before the trial began, various meetings were held with the agencies involved to explain the initiative and to try to set up a standardised procedure. Given the significance of defence solicitors in the other two trials, it was rather disappointing that a demonstration of electronic monitoring which was arranged for them was attended only by three of these key actors. One crucial difference between Tower Bridge and the other two sites was that in the former only three stipendiary magistrates were likely to be involved in remand cases.

There was no centralised decision-making procedure for electronic monitoring recommendations set up by the police; uniformed police officers would identify potential participants and *wherever possible* these would be checked by the duty officer (unfortunately, it is not known how often such checking took place). The recommendations were then passed on to the CPS. Another problem arose here as the local CPS used agents in some cases and these would have to be aware of the monitoring procedures; it was agreed that agents would contact the CPS about any recommendation for monitoring which came up. The police were uneasy about the violation procedures which had evolved in the other two sites, whereby any minor level 1 violations which occurred between 11.00 p.m. and 7.30 a.m. would not be followed immediately by a routine telephone call; such a call would be made after 7.30. The original procedure was reinstated for Tower Bridge so that a phone call would be made after any level 1 violation. The police were prepared to accompany service operators on visits to check on defendants, and requested that anyone whom they perceived as a special case should be followed up immediately. The boundaries of the trial area covered the jurisdiction of the magistrates' court and encompassed seven police stations—Southwark, Lewisham, Peckham, Deptford, Rotherhithe, Brockley and Tower Bridge.

There was little evidence of advance preparations for the trial by the police. However, unlike the other two trials, two defendants were accepted for electronic monitoring on the first morning; interestingly, both were charged with robbery. The police in the cell block were clearly unsure of what to do and who should be doing it, but the service operator dealt with matters efficiently speaking to the landlord of the defendants' flat and contacting British Telecom (this was the first time that two defendants were monitored together in the same residence). The induction procedure was not satisfactory as the police would not permit the operator to go into the cell to explain the system to the defendants, and this had to be done through a window in the cell door. As a telephone had to be installed the two participants were remanded into custody overnight, one to Feltham remand centre and the other to Wormwood Scrubs. Both defendants were fitted with the bracelet at these establishments as it was not possible to bring them back to the court cell block for this. Procedures at the two establishments went smoothly and prison staff were helpful, even though staff at Feltham had not been briefed about the trial. The curfew period of the defendants was set between 6.00 p.m. and 8.00 a.m. every day as they had had jobs when they were charged—but were now unemployed; it should be noted that the operators were under no obligation to bring such matters to the attention of the court.

The defendants' residence had a 'key' system budget meter which meant that when credit expired the power supply was cut off and a violation would be reported. The operators were not worried about this as the signals from both bracelets would be cut off at the same time and it was agreed that a violation report would not be completed. A few weeks later a problem arose with this situation. The electricity ran out and the defendants claimed that they could not afford to pay to have it switched on again. This was found in court not to be a breach of their bail conditions as a continuous supply of electricity was not mentioned in the agreement form. The Electronic Monitoring Agreement was amended to include the requirement to provide a continuous supply of electricity. During the first night of monitoring there were three level 1 violations which the defendants claimed were 'deadspots' in the bathroom; this was subsequently found to be the case and the problem was resolved.

Four weeks into the trial a total of six defendants had been monitored and several important issues had arisen. It was evident that the magistrates were interpreting the selection criteria rather differently from those in Nottingham and North Tyneside; in Tower Bridge alleged robbers were being monitored. Both the police and the CPS explained this by pointing out that burglars were normally granted bail at Tower Bridge (they were more likely to be remanded in custody at the other two sites), and therefore the bottom rung of the remand population started with those charged with robbery and these would comprise the potential target-group for electronic monitoring. Neither the police nor the CPS had made any recommendations for monitoring, and the police view was that those who were being granted bail subject to electronic monitoring were a danger to public safety.

The question of accommodation remained an (unproven) issue and a Home Office official discussed the possibility of utilising beds in two local Salvation Army hostels with representatives from the Army. This came to nothing as it was considered that the lay-out of the hostels was not conducive to electronic monitoring, and one of the rules of the hostels was that residents should not be in the building during the day—which would have implications for the setting of curfews.

A major problem arose over outstanding warrants—where a defendant was wanted for alleged crimes and due to appear at another court. No-one was sure how this situation should be dealt with, but all were agreed that it was a waste of time to bail someone subject to electronic monitoring who was liable to be arrested for appearance at another court as soon as he stepped outside of the Tower Bridge courtroom. Eventually, this was resolved and those who were monitored but also wanted at other courts had their warrants transferred to Tower Bridge, or they were permitted an approved absence to appear at the other court.

Concerns also arose over the decisions of some magistrates. In one case a defendant who had committed 37 alleged level 1 and four level 2 violations was arrested by the police. In court it was argued that all the recorded violations had been the result of equipment malfunctions (some had certainly been so caused) and the defendant was again granted bail with electronic monitoring. There were special circumstances which were agreed to have contributed to this decision: the case was heard on a Saturday and the CPS did not have access to the original papers; the Chubb duty officer's evidence was not accepted but treated as hearsay; and the case was heard by a visiting magistrate who was not familiar with the details of the trial. Another magistrate had granted conditional bail to five defendants who had been trying to arrange suitable accommodation in order to be accepted for monitoring. When they had not found a suitable residence, they were granted bail as the magistrate considered that it was unfair to exclude them from bail just because of their failure to find accommodation. Decisions such as these led to increased police concern; they felt that defendants charged with serious offences were being treated altogether too leniently, and their concerns would not have been lessened even if more stringent curfews had been imposed.

The first two defendants to be monitored had been interviewed for a television programme and had been paid for this; as soon as they had received payment they had taken off their bracelets and absconded. The responsibility of the media, who were taking more interest in this trial because it was based in London, thus became an issue.

By this time too, the violation procedures had been changed so that any overnight violations of up to 30 minutes were not followed up with the defendant between midnight and 6.30 a.m. For any violations over 30 minutes the police were to be contacted immediately.

It seems that for the first three weeks of the trial one of the original two defendants had not been monitored at all due to the system operators' misunderstanding the computer-generated coded printouts. The defendant had been arrested drunk in someone's garden during his approved absence. He was kept in police custody overnight and released the following day. When the custody sergeant mentioned this to the service operators they knew nothing about it. A careful check of the system, however, found that the coded printouts had indicated that the defendant was not being monitored, but that these printouts had been consistently misinterpreted due to their complexity.

By the end of January, roughly half-way through the trial, 16 defendants had been monitored; all of these had been recommended by defence solicitors, and one had been accepted at Crown Court. One defendant had been unable to participate because a telephone could not be connected to his home. To provide a line, British Telecom would have had to undertake major road excavations which would have taken four weeks. The service operators explained this in writing to the magistrate and the defendant was eventually remanded in custody.

In February a defendant who was being monitored cut off his bracelet and absconded; he was subsequently arrested by the police and charged with murder. This was the most serious incident which occurred during any of the trials; it was seen to have an effect upon the motivation of the magistrates who became considerably more apprehensive about the public safety aspects of electronic monitoring. Problems about the validity of information given to magistrates had also appeared; one defendant had forged letters from employers in an effort to have his curfew period changed; another had agreed to keep away from his victim as a condition of bail, but he was still living with the person. There were still difficulties in communication and the operators complained that if a monitored defendant was arrested in another area and held in custody they were often the last to hear about it; these cases were viewed as violations.

For the last eight weeks of the trial no new defendants were monitored, partly perhaps as a result of the alleged murder and partly due to the announcement of the run-down of the trial. The Tower Bridge trial ended as planned on 7 April. There had been a total of 37 recommendations for electronic monitoring, and all but one of these had occurred in the magistrates' court. 18 defendants in all were monitored, one of these in the Crown Court. Unusually, a large number of recommendations came from the magistrates—14 in all—while the remainder were from defence solicitors.

The role each of the agencies played in the trial will now be discussed.

The police

The police made no recommendations for electronic monitoring, and soon after the beginning of the trial made it clear that they had no intention of doing so. Public safety was the critical factor as far as they were concerned. It appears that they were not content with bail decisions prior to the trial, considering that too many defendants charged with serious offences were being granted bail. As the aim of the trial was to keep out of custody those who would have been remanded but for electronic monitoring, and as this approach was likely to mean that bail was granted to those charged with even more serious offences, their apprehensions are understandable. Such concerns will have coloured police attitudes towards the trial as a whole. Training and information seemed to be minimal and it is perhaps symptomatic that the liaison officer was on holiday for the first week of the trial. A surprising number of police officers who were seen during fieldwork seems to have no idea about the trial at all.

But even if the police had been more interested in supporting the electronic monitoring trial there would have been difficulties. The Metropolitan Police are a busy force and the police stations included in the trial area were in what is considered to be a notoriously high-crime area. Co-ordinating officers in seven stations would have been no easy matter, but it is unfortunate that no effort was made in this direction.

Because the area and many of its inhabitants were considered to be dangerous, the police attended checks on monitored defendants with the service operators. This work was not seen as especially demanding in resource terms, although if more defendants had been monitored it might have become so. It was also made clear that such co-operation might cease if too many defendants were treated leniently by the courts (in a few cases defendants who were monitored were arrested by the police and granted bail again under the same conditions). The police also commented upon the time which was wasted in responding to false alarms when tamper-alert mechanisms failed. It was noted that police follow-up visits decreased when one defendant, who had recorded 50 violations, absconded. They also wanted to know of violations lasting more than 30 minutes, which was not the case at the other two sites.

The police were satisfied with the service operators and the way they had carried out their tasks. They agreed to inform operators whenever a monitored defendant was arrested, but this was not a simple matter—especially if the arrest took place in a police division outside the trial area.

On the whole, the police claimed to be in favour of electronic monitoring (but they were opposed to any extension of the trial beyond its six months), though they did not feel it had worked in Tower Bridge because of the type of person who was monitored. If it was to be used as a condition of bail to monitor a curfew, rather than restricted to those who would have been remanded in custody, then it would be more successful.

The CPS

The role of the CPS in the Tower Bridge trial in terms of generating recommendations for monitoring was very limited—as it was in the other two trials. The CPS agreed to review all police recommendations for monitoring (a simple task as there were none), but made it clear that they would not take an active role in making recommendations themselves. They would advise the magistrates—and did so—in cases where monitoring was recommended by defence solicitors, but such advice was not seen to be positively encouraging or discouraging monitoring and each case was treated on its merits. The CPS approach was slightly complicated by the use of agents, but given its passivity this did not create any serious obstacles.

The CPS were helpful in liaising with the service operators; they informed the Chubb staff of the date and time of monitored defendants' next appearance at court, or when a case was brought forward or discontinued (both of which could result in violations being recorded). Cases heard at other courts, however, could pose problems in this respect. Prosecutors were aware of the more serious nature of the charges of those monitored at Tower Bridge, but pointed out that this resulted directly from the way bail was normally used. The CPS liaison representative was quite certain that monitoring was being used as an alternative to a remand in custody.

The courts

The task of the clerks at Tower Bridge was considerably simpler than at the other two trial sites due to the fact that only three stipendiary magistrates were likely to be involved in the remand courts. The senior clerk, while remaining slightly sceptical about the advantages of electronic monitoring (particularly the equipment), was very positive in her approach to the trial. She was quick to notice any potential problems: the lack of involvement of the Crown Court could lead to a different approach being taken there, which might lead to the overturning of magistrates' decisions; the difficulties which could arise as a result of the decision to grant conditional bail to defendants who could not arrange suitable accommodation for electronic monitoring. Ultimately, she considered electronic monitoring to be a useful option, though she remained dubious about the reliability of the equipment.

Perhaps the key feature of the trial was the presence of three stipendiary magistrates, although whether their professionalism, the fact that there were only three, or (perhaps most likely) a combination of these two factors was the most significant factor cannot be ascertained. Tower Bridge was unique in that 14 of the 36 recommendations came from the magistrates themselves who seemed to be keen to consider the possibility of electronic monitoring whenever they could. It is notable that when decisions were made which were inconsistent with the approach adopted, they tended to be taken by other magistrates than the three who normally dealt with cases; these three stipendiaries were interviewed.

None of the three seemed to think that electronic monitoring had made any significant difference to their decision-making; they took it into account whenever possible as they wished to keep defendants out of custody, but they dealt with serious cases and the risk was high. They agreed that there had been little in the way of guideline information from the Home Office and that in any case it was up to them to make the decisions. They were particularly unhappy about what they considered to be Home Office interference[1] with one decision about monitoring, and it was suggested that the Home Office did not appreciate the practical application of the system. All three had been responsible for granting bail with a condition of electronic monitoring to defendants, but had tried to choose those who would not present any threat to public safety and who would otherwise have been remanded in custody. The respondent who had bailed the defendant who had absconded and was subsequently charged with murder stated that this experience had changed his views about monitoring quite considerably. No obvious advantages were seen to apply to monitoring, though one respondent suggested that it would be more appropriate to use it simply to monitor a curfew as a normal condition of bail. Monitoring was not seen to provide a practicable alternative to a remand in custody, and the issue of alleged violations and how to ensure that these were real—as opposed to equipment failures—was mentioned as causing difficulties. Domestic burglars were seen as appropriate for monitoring, and the importance of having a family was commented upon (although it was also noted that the effect of monitoring on a family had to be considered). Finally, none of the three saw any place for electronic monitoring in the criminal justice system; they thought it had not been a success for remand cases (although some probation involvement might have helped) and that it certainly would not work as a sentence.

Procedures were set up for the use of monitoring in the Crown Court, but these were not tested to any real degree as only one person was granted bail subject to electronic monitoring.

The service providers

The problems which had been encountered during the acceptance tests with the Chubb performance seemed to spill over into the first few weeks of the trial; the documentation was not being completed correctly, it was being sent to the wrong place, and there had been a major equipment failure. As a result, Chubb became liable for liquidated damages of 25 per cent of the first month's payment. Despite these problems, the Chubb staff dealt well with the first few cases to be monitored when others were unsure or did not know the ropes; they handled both British Telecom and two prison establishments effectively. The other agencies, too, were impressed with the performance of the operators.

There were several difficulties faced by the operators in this site, all of which originated to some extent from the size of London: operators had to travel to prison establishments to fit bracelets to defendants; arrangements had to be made with the police and the CPS for the operators to be informed of

[1] This 'interference' was due to a breakdown in communication between the court and the Home Office. A Home Office official had instructed the service operators not to fit a defendant with a bracelet if there was a warrant outstanding for his arrest in another jurisdiction until an appropriate response to this situation had been properly worked out; the Justices' Clerk, however, had not been informed of this and she and the magistrates therefore perceived it as 'interference'. The matter was resolved (see p. 37).

appearances at court or arrests of those monitored; decisions had to be taken about whether or not to accept defendants who were wanted elsewhere on outstanding warrants. All of these issues were resolved to the degree that the trial ran satisfactorily. The operators themselves drove to their residences any defendants who had been put on the system at prison establishments if they were within their curfew period.

The Chubb operators seemed to be of a higher calibre than those used in the other two trials. Morale seemed to be low for the first few months when nothing appeared to be going well, but after this everyone cheered up and began to enjoy the job. One of the staff felt that a much wider range of skills was needed to do the job properly than had been suspected; and that good communication/interaction skills were crucial.

The Tower Bridge trial ran for 37 weeks (the original 24 plus 13 weeks to deal with cases), and most of the equipment failures came from tamper-alert mechanisms and deadspots.

34	—	tamper alert mechanism failures
25	—	possible deadspots
9	—	other Home Unit failures
7	—	transmitter battery failures
3	—	transmitter failures (possibly waterlogged)
3	—	other transmitter failures
2	—	reprogrammed Home Unit for GMT
1	—	BT line fault (other than 0800)
84		

Others involved

There is little to say about the other organisations involved in the trial. The Inner London Probation Service nominated a senior probation officer to sit on the local liaison committee. The SPO took a keen interest in the trial and noted that there was no evidence that electronic monitoring had resulted in defendants refusing to comply with probation orders; nor had any defendants approached the probation service about problems associated with monitoring. No-one had any complaints about British Telecom. Because of their rules and type of accommodation the two Salvation Army hostels had felt that they could not participate in the trial. And all dealings with prison establishments had gone smoothly, despite the fact that staff in one establishment had, mistakenly, not been notified of the trial.

Again, defence solicitors made the bulk of recommendations for electronic monitoring—23 out of 37—but their contribution was slightly lower than at North Tyneside. It is impossible to say how well-informed defence solicitors were about monitoring, but one of the stipendiaries considered that defence solicitors did not bring it up very often and only when they felt that custody was absolutely certain.

5 The results of monitoring

In a trial of this nature it was considered essential to collect information on who was being recommended for monitoring and by whom, who was actually monitored, curfew hours, bail failures and so on. Although their workload was increased by the introduction of electronic monitoring, the various agencies agreed to collect such basic information for the duration of the trials.

In all, a total of 50 defendants were monitored during the trials. Almost all of these had been previously remanded in custody, and the remainder had been held overnight by the police; this would suggest that it is almost certain that electronic monitoring was used as an alternative to a remand in custody for all cases. The 50 defendants were almost equally distributed amongst the three areas. Table 1 shows the overall situation at the end of the trials for all those monitored.

Table 1

Defendants monitored by area and outcome

	Total monitored(1)	*Sentenced*	*Violation*(2)	*Further offence*	*Bailed*(3)	*Other*(4)
Nottingham	17	4	3	6	1	3
N Tyneside	15	2	8	1	3	1
Tower Bridge	18	2	6	4	1	3
	50	8	18	11	6	7

(1) One defendant who was bailed subject to electronic monitoring at both magistrates' court and Crown Court has been counted twice.
(2) Includes two defendants who absconded and had not been re-arrested by the end of the trials.
(3) Following change of circumstances (eg variation of charge), defendants were bailed.
(4) Includes three cases where charges were withdrawn and one where the defendant was found not guilty.

On completion of the trials eight defendants had completed a period of electronic monitoring and been sentenced; five of these had received custodial sentences (two for three years, one for 18 months, one for 12 months, and one for three months), two received two year probation orders, and one received a community service order. More than half of those monitored (29 in all) violated their curfews or were charged with a new offence, and it may be significant that curfew violations were more numerous than new offences. It is conceivable that the novelty of electronic monitoring and the publicity surrounding its introduction may have encouraged in some defendants a feeling that the technology was not foolproof; this, however, is speculation.

Charts 1 and 2 show the flow of monitored cases in the three areas during the duration of the trials. Chart 1 shows the number of new monitoring cases per four week period at each of the trial sites; the greatest number of new cases in any period was six and this was reached twice at Tower Bridge, and on one occasion at Nottingham and North Tyneside. There were no new participants at North Tyneside between weeks 10 and 17, and Tower Bridge had no new cases after week 16. Chart 2 sets out the total number of defendants being monitored for each week of the trial in each area. A peak of eight persons was reached in Nottingham at weeks 8 and 9, and at North Tyneside a peak of six was reached in weeks 8, 10 and 11, after which numbers declined. At Tower Bridge, numbers rose steadily to a peak of 11 in weeks 16 and 17, declining thereafter.

Table 2 sets out the sources of recommendations for electronic monitoring and how often these were successful. 124 recommendations originated at the magistrates' court and 16 at Crown Court; the bulk of recommendations came from defence solicitors (105 out of 140, although those most likely to be successful were from magistrates, where 18 recommendations were made and 14 were accepted.

Most of the recommendations for monitoring were refused and Table 3 shows the reasons for refusal. In 21 cases bail was granted, while in the remaining cases defendants were remanded in custody. The availability of suitable accommodation had been considered as a potential problem both before the trials began and during them, but this was only mentioned as a problem in three cases.

Although the number of defendants monitored was similar in each of the three areas, the use of monitoring as a proportion of those remanded in custody seems to have differed widely. By using estimates of the numbers remanded into custody for each of the three magistrates' courts, it can be seen from Table 4 that monitoring was most likely to be used in North Tyneside (15 cases monitored and 41 remanded in custody) and least likely to be used in Nottingham (17 cases monitored and 209 remanded). But the use of monitoring did not seem to be related to the offences with which defendants had been charged; in Nottingham and North Tyneside the most frequent offence group was 'Other' which consisted mainly of motoring offences, while in Tower Bridge almost 90 per cent of those monitored (16 out of 18) were charged with offences of violence, burglary or robbery (this difference will be a result of different patterns of offending in each area which lead to different bail and remand practice generally).

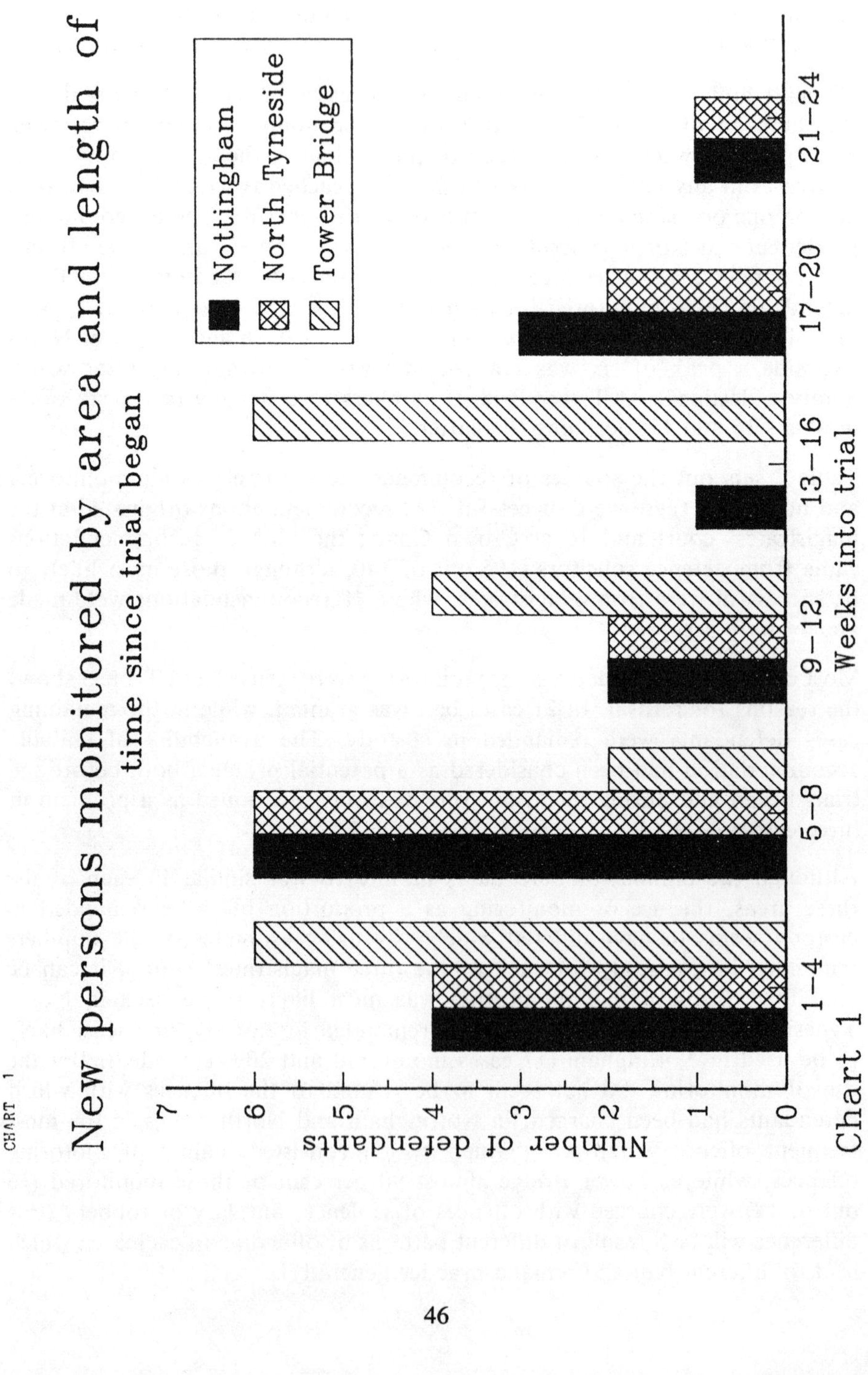
CHART 1
New persons monitored by area and length of
time since trial began
Nottingham
North Tyneside
Tower Bridge
Number of defendants
0
1
2
3
4
5
6
7
1–4
5–8
9–12
13–16
17–20
21–24
Weeks into trial
Chart 1

CHART 2

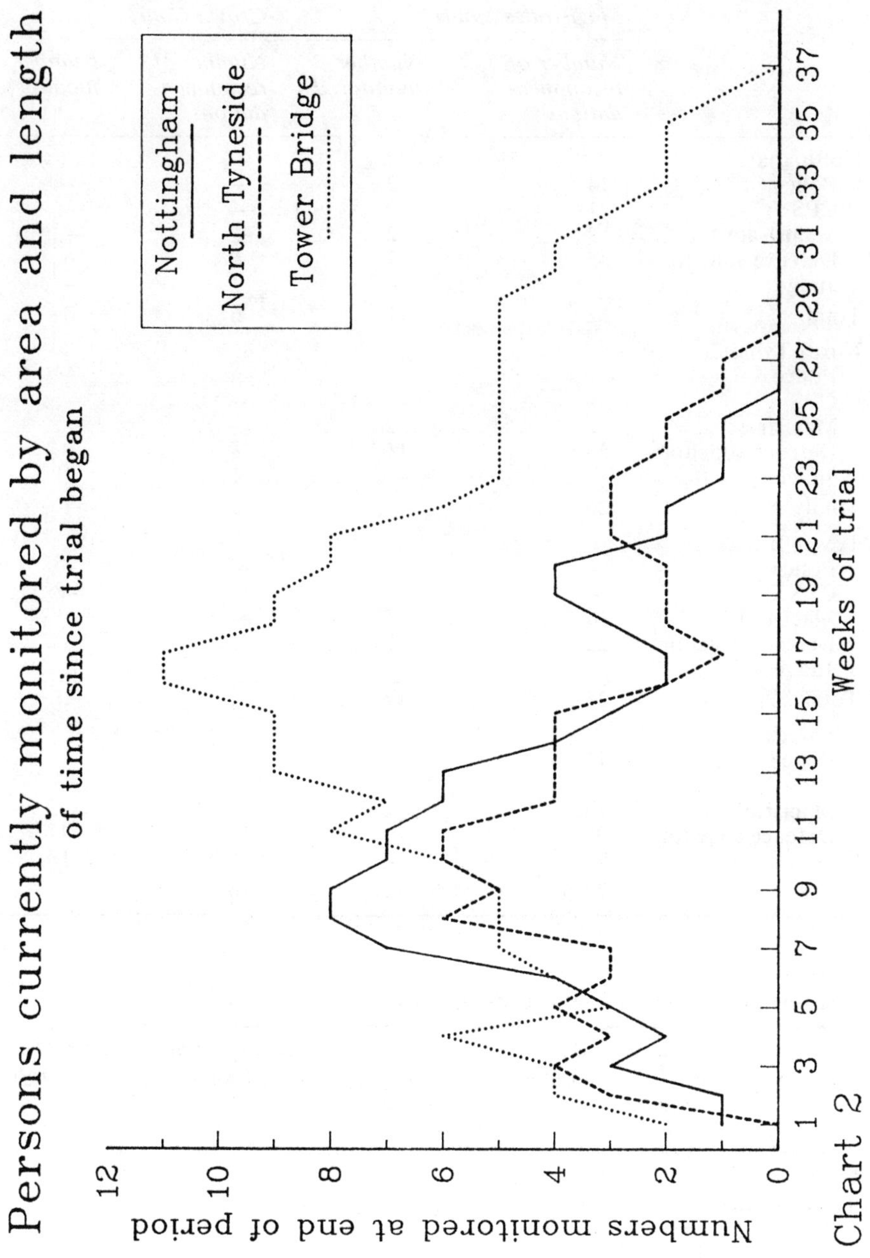
Persons currently monitored by area and length
of time since trial began
Nottingham
North Tyneside
Tower Bridge
Numbers monitored at end of period
12
10
8
6
4
2
0
1 3 5 7 9 11 13 15 17 19 21 23 25 27 29 31 33 35 37
Weeks of trial
Chart 2

Table 2

Recommendations for monitoring by agency recommending

	Magistrates' court		*Crown Court*	
	Number of recommen-dations	*Number monitored*	*Number of recommen-dations*	*Number monitored*
Nottingham				
Police	14	2	—	—
CPS	1	0	—	—
Magistrate	2	2	—	—
Defence solicitor	45	7	6	6
Judge	—	—	—	—
Total	62	11	6	6
North Tyneside				
Police	1	1	—	—
CPS	—	—	—	—
Magistrate	2	2	—	—
Defence solicitor	23	11	8	0
Judge	—	—	1	1
Total	26	14	9	1
Tower Bridge				
Police	—	—	—	—
CPS	—	—	—	—
Magistrate	14	10	—	—
Defence solicitor	22	7	1	1
Judge	—	—	—	—
Total	36	17	1	1
All areas				
Police	15	3	—	—
CPS	1	0	—	—
Magistrate	18	14	—	—
Defence solicitor	90	25	15	7
Judge	—	—	1	1
Total	124	42	16	8

Table 3

Reasons for refusing recommendations for monitoring by area

	Offence too serious	*Likely to re-offend*	*Accommo-dation unsuitable*	*Living outside area*	*Granted bail*	*Other*(1)	*Total refused*
Nottingham	7	10	2	—	16	16	51
N Tyneside	5	5	—	2	5	3	20
Tower Bridge	4	5	1	4	—	5	19
Total	16	20	3	6	21	24	90

(1) Includes 11 cases where the reason was unknown, 5 where there was no third party agreement to monitoring, 4 where the defendant was deemed to be 'unsuitable', and 2 where the defendant declined to be monitored.

Table 4

Defendants remanded in custody and monitored by offence group and area

Offence group	*Nottingham*		*N Tyneside*		*Tower Bridge*	
	Remanded	*Monitored*	*Remanded*	*Monitored*	*Remanded*	*Monitored*
Violence	32	3	8	1	15	4
Sex	7	—	3	—	10	—
Burglary	78	6	19	4	17	7
Robbery	20	—	1	3	17	5
Theft/ handling	33	—	3	—	7	1
Other	39	8	7	7	31	1
Total	209	17	41	15	97	18

All of those monitored during the trials were male (one recommendation, which was not accepted, was for a female); 19 were aged between 17 and 20, 15 were between 21 and 25 and the remaining 16 were between 26 and 47. Detailed information on the previous criminal history of defendants was not available, but more than half of those monitored were known to have been discharged from a custodial sentence within the previous three years.

Courts were able to monitor defendants for up to 24 hours per day, and two defendants—both bailed from Nottingham Crown Court—had such a curfew. Table 5 shows the curfew periods for defendants.

Table 5

Periods of electronic monitoring per day

	8–12 hrs	*12–16 hrs*	*16–23 hrs*	*24 hrs*	*Total monitored*
Nottingham					
Magistrates' court	5	1	5	—	11
Crown Court	—	—	4	2	6
N Tyneside					
Magistrates' court	1	4	9	—	14
Crown Court	—	1	—	—	1
Tower Bridge					
Magistrates' court	3	6	8	—	17
Crown Court	1	—	—	—	1
Total					
Magistrates court	9	11	22	—	42
Crown Court	1	1	4	2	8

Although defendants at Tower Bridge tended to be charged with more serious offences than those in the other two areas, this was not reflected in the curfew periods imposed. Of the three magistrates' courts, North Tyneside was the most stringent in terms of curfews with more than half being for 16 hours or more; in Nottingham and Tower Bridge just under half of the curfews were for this period. It is noticeable that curfew periods imposed at the Crown Courts tended to be longer than those used at the magistrates' courts.

Curfew periods could, of course, be changed and 20 amendments were made to approved absences from electronic monitoring; four of these were in Nottingham, nine in North Tyneside, and seven in Tower Bridge. All such amendments lowered the curfew period enabling defendants to look for and take up employment, to complete community service orders, to work overtime, etc. Defendants were also granted absences on specific dates for visits to hospitals and appearances in court.

Violations which involved absconding and those where further offences were alleged were shown in Table 1 (above), but there were also 217 other alleged violations and Table 6 sets out the details.

Table 6

Other violations of electronic monitoring by area

	30 mins	*30–60 mins*	*60–120 mins*	*120+ mins*	*Tamper alert*(1)	*Total*
Nottingham	73	5	2	7	—	87
N Tyneside	26	3	5	6	7	47
Tower Bridge	38	20	5	18	2	83
	137	28	12	31	9	217

(1) A tamper alert was not available in Nottingham

The majority of time violations (63 per cent) were for periods of less than 30 minutes (indeed 12 per cent were for periods of less than five minutes). Many of these violations were a result of defendants testing the system or poor time keeping. The average number of time violations per monitored defendant differed amongst areas: in Nottingham it was 5.1, in North Tyneside 3.1, and in Tower Bridge 4.6 (the Tower Bridge figure has been inflated because of one defendant who had 28 violations before absconding). Tamper alert mechanisms were used on the bracelet in North Tyneside and Tower Bridge, and seven alerts were recorded in the former area and two in the latter.

There was no clear relationship between further alleged offences or absconding and the age of defendants, the number of weeks for which they had been monitored, or the length of the curfew period.

It is difficult to draw any clear conclusions from these data. The numbers involved are low and the monitoring system was different in each of the three areas. There would appear to have been a high level of absconding and further offending, but it should be remembered that we have no control group with which to compare those monitored, there are no accurate studies of offending and absconding while on bail, and the defendants monitored represent a high-risk group insofar as they were fairly young (two-thirds were between 17 and 25) and more than half had had experience of custody. The presence of a tamper alert mechanism on the transmitter-bracelet does not appear to have had any effect upon the number of violations. One point which does seem to be reasonably clear, however, is that electronic monitoring was used as an alternative to a remand in custody during the trials.

6 Defendants' views on electronic monitoring

The views of defendants and offenders are only rarely considered in studies of the criminal justice system. There appears to be a certain unspoken agreement that having been sentenced to a disposal, or bailed with certain conditions, or remanded in custody, the views of the individual so dealt with are irrelevant. It may be that such people are difficult to contact, may be reluctant to be interviewed, and their views may be coloured by personal animosities towards representatives of the system. But the views of those who, in a sense, constitute the raw material of the criminal justice system should not be ignored and are just as relevant as those of any others. This is particularly so in the case of an initiative such as electronic monitoring. There would have been a serious gap in the research if some attempt had not been made to elicit the views of some of those who were bailed subject to electronic monitoring.

During the three trials a total of 20 defendants who had been monitored (40 per cent of all those mentioned) were interviewed in an effort to find out how they felt about it all. It had been hoped to see rather more than this, but it proved to be surprisingly difficult to locate potential respondents; some were still being monitored, but others had been sentenced, rearrested, or had absconded; and it was time-consuming to track down and arrange an interview with a defendant who had been subsequently either remanded in, or sentenced to, custody. Eight of the respondents were from Nottingham, five from North Tyneside, and seven from Tower Bridge; all were male and aged between 17 and 33 years old. On the whole, the offences with which respondents had been charged tended to be representative of the charges faced by those monitored in each area. There were no clear differences in views about electronic monitoring with regard to the trial area, the ages of respondents, or their charges.

The interviews were semi-structured, allowing the defendant to expand on and introduce topics which he felt were of particular importance in this context, but also ensuring that certain key subjects were covered. These included the method by which the defendant became aware of the option of electronic monitoring as a condition of bail and his decision to take part; his appreciation of the monitoring service provided and his relationship with the ground-level monitoring staff; and his personal and practical experience of wearing the monitor. Seven of the interviews were carried out in prison, either because the defendant's trial had taken place and he had been sentenced to custody (two cases), or because the participant had been re-arrested and remanded in custody following further offences while being monitored (five cases). One respondent was interviewed at the hostel in which he was residing for the purposes of electronic monitoring. He, in fact, absconded some weeks after the interview and was later rearrested and remanded in custody. Of the twelve remaining participants interviewed in their homes while being monitored, a further two also subsequently absconded and reoffended. This reflects the general rate of alleged serious violations within the total population of those monitored, over half of whom were alleged to have offended or absconded.

Interviews took approximately 40 minutes and participants had been electronically monitored for an average of seven weeks when interviewed; eight respondents had been monitored for between 2–4 weeks, six for between 5–8 weeks, and six for between 10–12 weeks. There were no discernible differences in views about monitoring with respect to the length of time respondents had been monitored. Three quarters of those interviewed were on a monitored curfew of 15 hours and above (one being on a 24 hour curfew). Others were on curfews of between 11 and 14 hours. (This reflects the curfew time on weekdays, and was often lengthened at weekends). There was a general feeling of discontent about the length of these curfews amongst the respondents. Many were interviewed in the presence of some members of their family and, though this was due to necessity rather than choice, it was nonetheless often very informative, as partners or parents often contributed their views on the system during the course of the interview.

The remainder of this chapter will describe the results of the interviews. It is important to stress that, because the sample is small, the findings reported here are merely suggestive of what the experience of monitoring as a condition of bail was like.

The decision process

The majority of those interviewed first heard of the possibility of being monitored from their defence solicitors—a quarter of the respondents were already on remand when this was suggested. A further quarter had not consciously considered monitoring at all until it was suggested by the magistrate—these defendants were all from the Tower Bridge jurisdictions where stipendiary magistrates were in operation. The families of three of the defendants suggested monitoring to them, and others first heard about it from other inmates while on remand or through media publicity. Three respondents interviewed had been accepted for monitoring at the Crown Court as opposed to the magistrates' court and these had all heard about monitoring through discussion in the prison and on the radio. They appeared to have taken marginally more initiative in the decision process for monitoring as they asked their defence solicitors to make a 'judge in chambers' application for bail with a condition of electronic monitoring.

At this point it should be noted that most defendants appeared to have only a very vague notion of what monitoring was about. Quite often it was only suggested on the morning of the court appearance (or actually in court in the case of Tower Bridge). There was little time to discuss the system with family members, or those with whom the defendant would be residing, other than to have the third party agreement signed where necessary. In the haste to have a family member released from custody, it seems probable that there was little real understanding of the system on the part of co-habitees. Similarly, in the case of the defendants, regardless of the level of understanding their defence solicitors had about monitoring, very little information was imparted to the potential participants. This was not an issue to them however, typical responses were:

> I didn't really understand what it meant at the time, but I didn't care, I just wanted to get out.
>
> I didn't know. I didn't have a clue, I just knew it was a strap or something.
>
> I didn't know anything about it.

The first point in the process when the system of monitoring was explained in detail to the interviewees was when they were visited by the service suppliers for the induction process. This took place either in police custody at the cell blocks attached to the courts or at a remand centre and might be a day or two after the defendant had been recommended by the court for electronic monitoring. Although this was a potentially stressful experience for the defendants, none of them reported it as being so. The overwhelming view was that the service suppliers in all three areas were detailed and clear in their explanation of the whole monitoring process. All the equipment involved was explained in a very professional manner. Despite the rather worrying lack of knowledge about monitoring apparent at the time the defendants consented to it, when this was remedied by the service suppliers all but one respondent was still reasonably happy with the situation. The remaining respondent had had definite reservations about the system when it was explained to him, and claimed that he only accepted it because it was approaching Christmas and he wanted to be with his wife and children.

In sum then, it appears that neither defendants nor their solicitors had anything but the most superficial knowledge of how the electronic monitoring system worked at the time of consent. It seems that the decision was made purely on the basis that electronic monitoring provided a route to release from custody, and defendants—at least at this point in the process—were not particularly concerned about what it entailed, so long as they could obtain it.

Relationships with service suppliers

Thus, relationships with service suppliers tended to begin well and they remained positive. This was the case for all three areas in general, with the exception of one of the ground-level staff in the Tower Bridge trial who was reportedly somewhat brusque in manner according to three of the respondents there. In general, however, respondents described the teams as being polite, friendly and informative. Response to problems with hardware was quick, and by and large, service operators were not considered to be too keen to blame defendants for alleged violations. Approximately half of the interviewees did report getting fed up with continual problems with their hardware, particularly in the early days on the system, and the consequent increase in visits this caused. This problem was noted in all three areas.

Aside from these problems, a member of the service team would call once a week to check the equipment and deal with any problems the participant might have, as and when these arose. The ground-level staff in all three areas made it clear that they were merely supplying a service and were not a criminal justice agency, and this seemed to be accepted by respondents. Eight, however, felt that the system was intruding on their privacy and that they were constantly under scrutiny:

> It bugs me, every five minutes they keep coming around or phoning me up.

Although it should be emphasised that they had no definite complaints about the behaviour of the operators.

Conversely, however, just over half had no problems with feelings of intrusion at all (and this issue did not appear to be related to length of curfew). It should be pointed out that 'problems with the equipment' may be interpreted in two ways. They may have been genuine faults with hardware, and there is no doubt that this was the case to some extent. It was also possible, of course, that these problems were due to violations on the part of the defendant; either through tampering with the equipment or through absconding for short periods of time. Unfortunately, with the technology as it stands, there is some scope for debate about which of these applied; defendants were apt to blame the equipment, and service operators tended to suspect violations. (This was an issue which worried the police in particular).

It appears then, that though difficulties were experienced with the equipment, the participants were relatively satisfied with their treatment from the service suppliers, though the system as a whole was considered to be intrusive by about half.

Personal experiences of electronic monitoring

How did defendants feel about being monitored? Were they satisfied that they had made the right choice in agreeing to it? How restrictive did they think it was? What were the advantages and disadvantages?

The overwhelming feeling which emerged from this line of questioning was a strong sense of restriction of liberty—much more than respondents had expected. Eight interviewees went as far as to describe their experience of monitoring as akin to being a prisoner in their own home. Interestingly, six of these had particularly long curfew times of between 19 and 22 hours. Many of these respondents described their time on curfew as a mixture of boredom, frustration and temptation:

> I don't know, at times it makes you depressed you know. I've gone upstairs and laid down and just laid there depressed thinking well, I'm in prison anyway, but I've got to make the most of it.
>
> You're just being kept in custody in your own house really.

Most of these defendants still, however, marginally preferred monitoring to custody.

A further eight of the respondents found the experience of monitoring difficult and trying, but appreciated very much the freedom of their own home. The ability to wash, eat and sleep in their own time and in their own space was seen as a big advantage:

> I like to be around when things happen . . . you can't even cook your own meal inside.
>
> It's the comforts of home, isn't it? Better than being banged up, isn't it?

Two interviewees said that monitoring was more punitive than custody:

> It's just a wind up—I'd rather be inside . . . I've got an hour a day. Nine till ten in the morning. Sometimes I don't even get up. I haven't got a set routine. Like, in gaol I had a set routine then, I could go to the gym. Now I don't know what I'm doing. It just bores me.

This particular respondent was on a 23 hour curfew and was residing at a hostel, having been on remand for 10 months, and found the situation particularly intolerable. He later absconded and ended up remanded in custody again.

Three respondents in all (one of whom fell into the difficult but appreciative category) noted that the extra control exerted by wearing the monitor had helped them stick to their curfew and stay out of trouble:

> It's helping me to keep in and it's helping me to adapt in a way. I was used to going out until about 5 o'clock in the morning . . . it was leading to more crime, more charges, more prison.

And one of these noted the advantage of being out of prison because,

> . . . you're just mixing with criminals and you're learning new things . . . you come out worse than you went in.

Despite the obvious restriction of liberty, many greatly appreciated the fact that they could be with their families and friends. This was stated as the main advantage of electronic monitoring and it outweighed the fact that, had the defendants been remanded in custody, this time would be taken off any eventual custodial sentence. (The vast majority resided at home while on the monitoring system, either in the parental home or with partners and children). The reasons for this were largely obvious. Respondents reported having the company and support of their partners or parents, and being able to help with children and various other domestic and financial matters. It also allowed the two defendants who lived alone to retain their council flats. One respondent stated that:

> You do worry about the kids when you're on remand—how they are getting on, are they still going to school, but when you're tagged you can be with them and help them.

The experience of being at home, however, was sometimes a mixed blessing. Nearly half of the co-habitees of respondents were reported as seeing monitoring unreservedly as a positive thing; they were happy that their husband or son was at home, not just for the company, but also because of the fact that they knew their whereabouts and that the monitor would restrict them from any further trouble. Rather worryingly however, a similar number of co-habitees, according to the defendant's account, found the long curfews a definite strain after a time and sometimes a source of considerable friction. The wife of one respondent stated:

> Having my husband round the house all the time has really put a strain on things. We argue all the time and get on top of one another. We never go out and I keep going on at him because we never do anything with the kids and I'm stuck with them all the time. It's a pain in the neck.

Similarly, a younger participant living with his parents, who had written an essay on his experience of tagging reported that:

> When you're inside, you're inside. With the family, when you're round the house with your tag and you're getting fed up, you tend to take it out on the family and end up getting kicked out or something.

At least three of those who had signed a 'third party' agreement to permit defendants to reside with them whilst subject to monitoring later withdrew their consent, (two of these were parents), which resulted in the defendant being remanded in custody.

It would seem that friction between members of the family when one is undergoing electronic monitoring may be a potentially serious consequence of the system and must be considered (the availability of counselling and support would be useful in such circumstances). It would be misleading though, to paint a totally negative picture of these defendants' experiences of the process. A number, for instance, greatly appreciated being able to keep their jobs. As well as the financial advantages of this, they said that it gave them time away from home during which they felt productive and useful and this, in turn, made the curfew somewhat easier. As one interviewee put it:

> Well obviously I can get on with my life, I can work, I can go and buy little things for my flat, I can decorate my mum's house.

Another interviewee (who was subsequently sentenced to three years in custody for armed robbery) explained that:

> You're out earning a living and so not putting any financial difficulty on the state. It must cost them a fortune to keep me in here [prison]. You're still being useful.

Three participants, however, noted that it was very difficult to *obtain* employment while on electronic monitoring, mostly because of the longer curfew hours given if one was unemployed, but also due to the stigma associated with the monitor. Whether or not this is actually the case, it appears to have affected the participants' motivation with regard to job-hunting. The general feeling was that a prospective employer would be unlikely to take on someone who was being electronically monitored for an alleged crime and most respondents said they would try and conceal this fact:

> . . . because they'd think he must have done something really awful for that.

> Loads of people [have noticed the bracelet], especially at work. That's the main thing you've got to be careful of—if your employer sees it he wouldn't like it.

More specifically on the sensitive issue of stigmatisation, over half of those spoken to felt embarrassed about wearing the bracelet and did their best to cover it up in public (usually using a sock or a bandage), and sometimes from their children, though this would often be for practical reasons. One defendant's wife said:

> The kids want to cut it off, but I tell them the men will come and take Daddy away again.

In general, respondents did not mind too much if family and friends saw or knew about the bracelet, but were uneasy about strangers being aware of it. Many respondents considered that the bracelet became more visible in certain public situations, such as on a bus:

> It depends who it is that sees it. Like if I was sitting on the bus and someone saw it, that would worry me, but like friends and relatives it doesn't. When I sit down, I push my trousers down like that, so no-one sees it.

On the other hand, eight respondents were not at all concerned others noticing the monitor:

> No-one noticed it, I wouldn't have cared if anyone did anyway.

The Marconi monitor was large and easily visible to the eye. The Chubb monitor was smaller and neater, but black in colour and this made it conspicuous.

Turning to the practical issues of wearing the monitor, very few found it comfortable to wear, the vast majority claiming that it caused irritation or swelling or both and for some it actually cut the skin. Many participants had the monitor changed from leg to leg each week when the service supplier visited, in order to give one ankle a rest. Many also claimed to find the monitor clumsy and that they bumped into things with it in the course of daily household activities. One claimed that it interfered with his sexual behaviour!

> It [the monitor] used to upset her [girlfriend] with the light on. You know, you've got a big square box when you jump into bed with that on your leg. I had to watch myself in bed with it. During sexual activities it used to work itself loose.

Over a third did note, however, that after a period of time they became accustomed to wearing the bracelet:

> You do get used to it. When I first got it on, it felt really awkward—sliding up and down your leg. By the time I got home it had cut into my ankle. I had to have it changed to my left leg so I went through it all again. After a while you do get used to it though, half the time you forget it's there.

Respondents were asked if in general they considered electronic monitoring to be closer to remand in custody or bail with conditions (only one respondent had been charged with his first offence and thus had no experience of either). The message very strongly communicated was that it was much closer to remand in terms of restriction of liberty. Eleven respondents felt that the situation on monitoring became harder to bear as time went on, and said that they felt more and more temptation to abscond; seven of these either had already been re-arrested and charged with a further offence (including absconding), or were subsequently re-arrested. Of those who felt that temptation remained constant or actually diminished as time passed only four were re-arrested.

A total of 13 respondents were interviewed while still on the system; one-third said that they could not tolerate monitoring for more than a couple of months, one-third said it could be tolerated for a long time if conditions were better—if one had longer hours and a job, and one-third felt it could be tolerated for quite some time as it stood. 12 out of the 20, however, said that they would unreservedly volunteer for electronic monitoring if a similar situation arose in the future, claiming that even though it was hard, it was better than custody:

> I prefer electronic monitoring to custody, yes. At least I am at home and can sleep comfortably. It's not really much more freedom than custody, but at least you've got your own home to walk around in.

A further two said they would accept it again under better conditions. The remaining six stated that they would not accept monitoring again under any circumstances, if they had a choice; and that they had only accepted this time to see what it was like, but had found it too much to tolerate:

> . . . [I'd take] remand [in future] . . . I'm sick of wearing this thing . . . staying in all the time . . . it gets on me nerves . . . and on remand it comes off your sentence. I tried it just to see what it was like, but now I've tried it I wouldn't do it again.

Summing up then, it would seem that electronic monitoring was certainly not seen as an easy option by defendants. Even those who were willing to volunteer for monitoring if they were given the choice in the future spoke of problems. Electronic monitoring was seen as restrictive and closer to a remand in custody than to bail with conditions; but the advantages of being at home with one's family outweighed restricted freedom. Long curfews were considered to be particularly oppressive, and the importance of having a job was noted by several respondents. Domestic problems could also arise. It was clear from the interviews that adequate knowledge of the system and the difficulties it might pose were not available prior to consent. It is important that such potential problems should be communicated to candidates for monitoring and their families in order that they are fully aware of what might be involved. The service operators supplied a good deal of knowledge but this came a little too late; they were seen to be helpful and there were no signs of tension between them and defendants. The equipment, however, was not especially comfortable and improvements to the bracelet would seem to be necessary.

7 The technology of electronic monitoring

In this chapter the technology used in the trials will be described, its performance assessed, and the role of the service providers will also be discussed where this has not been touched upon in earlier chapters.

The technology used for electronic monitoring is relatively simple. It consists of a low-powered radio transmitter which is attached to the participant, and a receiver which uses a standard telephone line to pass information on to a central computer facility using an 0800 toll-free number. The receiver, or Home Unit, is connected between the telephone and the wall socket. Where defendants during the trials did not have a telephone, a call-barred telephone was installed which meant that only the telephone number of the central computer could be called by the defendant; and incoming calls could not be received unless these came from the service providers.

During the trials the service providers were asked to record all faults relating to the hardware, software and communications and send this information to the Home Office on a weekly basis.

The principal difference between the system used by Marconi and that used by Chubb was that the Marconi system had been used in the field at several sites in the USA for 18 months before the start of the trials in England. This did not, in the event, mean that the Marconi system was trouble-free; as has been noted, Marconi failed the first acceptance test at Nottingham because the equipment would not function over the British Telecom network, and there were continuous problems with the tamper alert mechanism for the first month of the North Tyneside trial. The software was poorly designed and seemed to be unnecessarily complicated; screen layouts were confusing and could result in operator error. The system was generally unfriendly, an a high level of operator training was needed—which was not commensurate with the amount of work involved.

The Chubb equipment was specially designed for the electronic monitoring trial and, therefore, had had no field use. It has already been noted that Chubb failed the first acceptance test partly because the equipment did not meet the required specification. Like the Marconi system, the applications software was unfriendly and difficult to use. Screen layout seemed to have been designed with little consideration for the user. The training requirement was far higher than should have been necessary, and the overall poor system design meant that operator error was almost certain to occur. There were a higher than expected number of false positive range violations at Tower

Bridge, but these were overcome by more careful siting of the Home Unit in the defendant's residence, and by the use of a twin aerial to overcome signal cancellation due to reflection of the signal from the transmitter. There were also problems with the tamper alert mechanism. Given the untested nature of the equipment, however, the number of faults was not excessive.

Overall, the performance of both the Marconi and Chubb teams was satisfactory, despite the difficulties with acceptance tests and a few incidents during the course of the trials. The performance of ground-level staff improved as the trials went on; they became more used to the equipment and to the tasks needed for the job in general. The response time to requests from the courts was prompt, and the average time to respond to an alleged violation was within the time stipulated in the contract. Each of the sites had no problems in handling the number of defendants who were monitored. Unfortunately, however, the low number of defendants who were accepted for monitoring was not sufficient to allow any meaningful assessment of the maximum number of defendants who could be handled effectively by each operator.

A brief ergonomic assessment of the transmitter-bracelets used in the trials was carried out and concluded that neither the Marconi nor Chubb transmitter was ergonomically acceptable.

In conclusion, the electronic monitoring systems (including the equipment and the manpower) worked adequately during the trials. But this is not to say that improvements could not be carried out for any future developments. Software in particular needs to be improved markedly; hardware to a lesser degree, but in this case there are continuous developments in technology which could be utilised in the future, eg a radio link between the Home Unit and the central computer would obviate the need to involve British Telecom, would therefore cost less than the phone system, and would mean that third party agreement to install a telephone would not be needed (telephone lines could still be used where a phone was available or radio communications could not be established). An ergonomically acceptable transmitter-bracelet should be specified and required for any future trial. And there is room for improvements in the training of staff, particularly using the lessons which have been learnt during the acceptance tests and the trials themselves.

8 Conclusions

It was apparent to all of those involved in the trials that it would be difficult to draw firm conclusions about their outcome; the short time-scale of six months and the small numbers monitored were always likely to be important factors in this respect. But the trials have thrown up a series of issues which will need to be taken into account in any further developments—and this is what was to be expected. The electronic monitoring 'experiment' was very much a test project, and therefore was always likely to be more useful in demonstrating the difficulties and obstacles which monitoring might face, than in providing definitive answers about how such difficulties might be overcome.

In this final chapter responses will be given to the four questions which the research originally aimed to answer.

Is electronic monitoring being used as an alternative to a remand in custody?

The short answer to this question is yes; almost all of those who were bailed subject to electronic monitoring had been remanded in custody prior to monitoring, and thus it may be concluded that electronic monitoring was indeed used as an alternative to a remand in custody (it is, of course, possible that some of the participants would have been bailed at some point, but this can only be hypothetical). Further evidence can be adduced to support this. Representatives of the criminal justice agencies in all three areas were sure that monitoring had been used as an alternative to a remand in custody. The difficulties faced by the police and CPS in finding suitable candidates for monitoring, and the lengthy deliberations which took place in court whenever monitoring was recommended can also be seen as providing some proof that the criterion about using electronic monitoring only for those who would otherwise have been remanded in custody was adhered to strictly.

But, as might be expected, there are complicating factors which should not be ignored. In the first place, the initiative was 'experimental' and thus carried out under artificial conditions; a great deal of effort was spent before the trials in trying to impress upon those who would be involved that it was vital that electronic monitoring should only be used as an alternative to a remand in custody, and this message continued to be reinforced as the trials progressed. It may be that if the alternative to custody message had not been hammered home so regularly, or if the trials had continued for a longer period, this criterion might not have been so strictly adhered to—but these are hypothetical issues.

Further, it should be noted that the available pool of potential candidates for electronic monitoring as an alternative to a remand in custody has been decreasing. The average remand population fell by eight per cent in 1989 (Home Office 1990), which may mean that defendants who previously would have been remanded in custody are now being granted bail by the courts. The rise in the number of bail information schemes operated by the probation service is also likely to lead to fewer defendants being remanded in custody. Ultimately, this may result in those who are remanded in custody being seen as an extreme group whose members cannot be bailed under any conditions for reasons of public safety.

How successful is monitoring as a condition of bail?

It is very difficult to provide an answer to this question. On the one hand, the majority of those monitored were charged with further offences or with absconding (which usually meant they were remanded in custody). Conversely, we have nothing against which this seemingly high level of violations can be compared, and those monitored would seem to be a fairly high-risk group in any event (about two-thirds were below the age of 25, and more than half had previous experience of custody; see Phillpotts and Lancucki 1979). It is unlikely that electronic monitoring would necessarily lead to a reduction in offending, but it might be expected to have an impact upon absconding and this does not seem to have happened.

There were also more than 200 time violations, 75 per cent of which lasted for less than one hour. Many of these were a result of bad time-keeping, or testing-out of the system, and it is possible that a few resulted from equipment failures which were not recorded as such. The novelty of electronic monitoring and the publicity surrounding the trials may have led, directly or indirectly, to so many time violations. The availability of monitoring did at least ensure that any minor breaches of curfew or absconding were detected quickly.

Another factor which has to be considered is the number of equipment failures. There can be little doubt that these have contributed to the number of alleged time violations, and they have also led to disagreements between service operators and defendants about whether or not an alleged violation was due to the defendant or to an equipment malfunction. Such disagreements in turn led to doubts from police officers about the efficacy of the equipment, and the confidence of the police in the equipment would seem to be a critical factor in their support of electronic monitoring. It should be noted, however, that most equipment failures occurred in the first half of each trial and that these fell away significantly during the second three months.

Most of those involved in the trials were not convinced of the success of monitoring as a condition of bail when used as an alternative to a custodial remand. They considered that if electronic monitoring had any future it was as just another condition of bail and not as an alternative to custody; or as part of a sentence where it might be used to monitor a curfew. Defendants who were interviewed, however, did seem to view it as a success; although they saw it as restrictive and closer to custody than bail with other conditions, they almost all preferred it to custody. Unfortunately, it was not possible to interview some of those defendants who were alleged to have turned down the chance of being monitored because they thought it would be too much trouble as it would not be deducted from any custodial sentence (as far as can be ascertained, there were not very many of these).

What are the practical issues involved in the use of electronic monitoring?

Perhaps the most significant points which have emerged from the three trials have been the need to try to ensure consistency in the decision-making process for electronic monitoring (which is not, of course, a new problem for the criminal justice system), and the difficulty in generating suitable recommendations for monitoring. The number of possible sources for recommendations for monitoring made it difficult to be sure that all were working to the same agenda; the police, the CPS, defence solicitors, magistrates, and judges. As it happened, defence solicitors were by far the most fruitful source of recommendations, but were also the most inaccessible in terms of being able to influence them to follow the guidelines. And defence solcitors' duty is to their clients, so that they may also be the most likely to depart from guidelines.

The police clearly did not find it easy to make recommendations for monitoring, and this was the case even in Nottingham where the bulk of police recommendations originated. First, there was something of a logical reversal necessary in deciding that bail would be opposed for a defendant and then deciding that bail could be granted subject to electronic monitoring. And second, the police awareness of public safety meant that they were always likely to err on the side of caution. If the police were to be involved in recommending candidates for monitoring then a filtering system such as was set up in Nottingham would seem to be vital.

The CPS role in the trials was disappointing in that they were virtually invisible in terms of recommendations (one out of 124). If monitoring were to be developed as a condition of bail, then greater CPS involvement would seem to be necessary.

Magistrates and judges generally did not seem to have much confidence in the applicability of electronic monitoring as an alternative to a remand in custody, and commented on the difficulties of finding suitable candidates for it. They were willing to countenance a trial with a limited time-span, but if monitoring were to be introduced on any national basis then much greater confidence in the system on the part of both these groups would be vital.

The performance of the service suppliers is another factor in the success of electronic monitoring. Those involved were satisfied with the way the operators carried out their work, and there is no doubt that this went much better than the acceptance tests might have suggested. It should be added, however, that the staff were never pushed particularly hard due to the low numbers monitored. There were equipment faults (and these caused problems for police and courts as well as defendants) which will need to be resolved. And it is clear that the ground-level staff need to be of high calibre—the ability to deal with various representatives of the criminal justice system as well as those subject to monitoring is essential—and adequate training must be provided.

Although lack of accommodation was thought to be one reason for the lack of recommendations, the provision of hostel beds in Nottingham did not lead to any increase in potential candidates. Hostel staff considered that such a residence was not ideal for monitoring and had only offered to help in order to try to keep people out of prison. Both defendants monitored in a hostel absconded; but this may have been partly a result of their particularly long curfews (23 and 24 hours) which may have exacerbated the hostel situation. Dormitory accommodation in a hostel is not thought to be suitable for electronic monitoring.

There was no clear relationship between the length of curfew and alleged violations, but long curfews were commented upon adversely by magistrates and defendants. A long curfew period could not only put further strain upon a relationship, but lead to problems in looking for work (and thus entitlement to benefit). Mature, responsible people with a family and job were considered to be ideal for electronic monitoring, but these are not characteristics associated with the kind of offenders dealt with during the trials. They were young and unemployed and perhaps lacked the self-discipline to cope with the demands of monitoring. The flexibility of monitoring a curfew could be more widely known; and this might be especially important with regard to employment.

One key point to note is that, generally, those who were monitored preferred it to custody though they also found it to be restrictive and demanding. A significant minority, however, said that they would not choose monitoring again; it was too rigorous and it would not be deducted from a custodial sentence. More knowledge for potential candidates in advance of consenting to be monitored would be helpful.

The need for probation involvement was seen to be crucial. Without any prompting, many of those involved in the trials mentioned how helpful probation officers might be. They could advise participants prior to any agreement to monitoring; they could help with accommodation problems; and they could provide counselling and support for those who were subject to monitoring. Bail information schemes could be used to provide assessments of suitability for electronic monitoring if probation service objections could be resolved.

Finally, the position of defendants who are subject to electronic monitoring with long curfews with regard to their entitlement to various welfare benefits needs to be clarified. This was not only a serious problem for some defendants, but may have inhibited some magistrates from using monitoring as much as they might have done.

How cost-effective is monitoring compared to other conditions of bail and to remands in custody?

In any cost-benefit analysis of electronic monitoring as a condition of bail a series of costs would have to be calculated. The total running costs of a scheme should be easily available (and this would have to include the costs of installing telephones if these formed part of the system). Various activities resulting from the monitoring process would have to be costed, preferably when these had become routine: police time in deciding whether or not to recommend for monitoring; CPS response to the police recommendation; the time taken to complete any relevant documentation; the costs of any lengthening of the time taken in court when electronic monitoring is considered. Where failures occur there will also be associated costs such as police time, court time, and time spent in custody if those who violate are remanded in custody. Other costs and benefits might also be considered such as those associated with the amount of freedom involved in electronic monitoring; and receipt of welfare benefits would have to be counted. Similar calculations would have to be made for two other groups—those who were remanded in custody, and those who were bailed with conditions. Key factors in comparing the groups would be the extent to which those who were monitored represented an alternative to a remand in custody, the numbers involved and the length of time for which monitoring was carried out.

The trials themselves could not be said to be cost-effective because of the low numbers monitored and the number of violations recorded, even though those monitored can be assumed to represent alternatives to custody. But it would be rather naïve to expect any kind of new initiative to prove to be cost-effective; a trial of any kind is likely to be more helpful in clarifying issues and pointing to problems rather than solving them. In this respect, it is significant that none of the police forces involved considered the trials to be a serious drain on resources; and the same can be said for the CPS (though this may change if they were to take a more positive role in monitoring). The time taken to hear cases in court took considerably longer, but this would be expected to move back towards the norm as everyone became more familiar with the process (and it is significant that the time taken by the stipendiary magistrates at Tower Bridge to hear bail applications where electronic monitoring was recommended did not increase).

This question, therefore, cannot be answered in any meaningful sense. It would be misleading to divide the total costs of the trials (around £700,000) by the total number of defendants monitored. Not only was a significant proportion of the costs of the trials made up of the capital costs of setting up the monitoring system (estimated to be at least 20 per cent of the costs);

but within the limited time-span of the trials the various agencies involved did not have the time to settle down to a 'normal' approach to electronic monitoring—this may have resulted in higher costs (perhaps another five–seven per cent of the costs). Taking these estimates into account, the running costs of the trials may have been nearer £500,000—but it should be emphasised that these are rough estimates and that the low number of defendants monitored would still mean that the system as tested in the trials was not cost-effective.

The development of a new policy can take various forms. One possible process takes the form of a new initiative being greeted by many of those who will be involved in its practical ramifications as providing the definitive solution to a critical problem. Expectations for the new policy are, therefore, raised artificially high and initial results tend to confirm these expectations. Later, more detailed studies demonstrate that the initiative cannot meet all of the expectations (and, indeed, should not have been expected to do so); disappointment results, a degree of backlash may begin and the initiative may become perceived as a complete failure when in fact it does have certain advantages. This is a somewhat crude outline of a complex process which may not be inevitable. There are some signs, however, that such a process may be taking place in the USA with regard to electronic monitoring, although it must be added that the use of monitoring continues to expand rapidly there.

It is less likely that such a process will take place in England and Wales. Most of those involved in the trials were sceptical about electronic monitoring, although they did see a place for it in the criminal justice system—albeit a relatively small place. And this may be where the major difficulty lies. If electronic monitoring is to be developed then it will surely be on a national basis. This will ensure that the costs of the system will be high. Given the low numbers deemed suitable for monitoring during the trials, and the moves towards individualised disposals for offenders which focus on their specific offences, will there be enough candidates to make electronic monitoring financially cost-effective?

Electronic Monitoring Agreement

I, the undersigned defendant, understand that I have been granted bail on condition that I agree to be electronically monitored and comply with the curfew and other conditions set out below.

1. I understand that I will be monitored through the use of electronics and computer technology and I agree to wear an ankle bracelet 24 hours a day until determination of my case in either the magistrates' court or Crown court.

2. I understand the court requires me to remain at my residence other than between the following times:

	out	in	out	in	out	in
Sunday	....	....	....	....	....	....
Monday	....	....	....	....	....	....
Tuesday	....	....	....	....	....	....
Wednesday	....	....	....	....	....	....
Thursday	....	....	....	....	....	....
Friday	....	....	....	....	....	....
Saturday	....	....	....	....	....	....

I understand that leaving my residence for any reason other than between the stated times is a breach of my condition of bail and may result in my arrest.

3. If I have to leave my residence because of an emergency I will first try to inform the service provider, but in any event I will report to the service provider as soon as possible to explain the circumstances. I understand that should such a situation arise a statement will be made to the police and that I may be required by them to verify the details.

4. I understand that the purpose of this monitoring equipment is to ensure my presence at my residence at all times except those specified in paragraph 2. I understand that the loss of a receiving signal (or the receipt of a tamper signal) at the central monitoring station will alert the service provider.

5. I understand that the removal or attempted removal of the bracelet is a violation of my condition of bail and may result in my arrest.

6. I agree to allow access to my residence by British Telecom and the service provider for the purpose of:

a) *installation and removal of a telephone if one does not already exist there;*
b) *installation and removal of electronic monitoring equipment;*
c) *maintenance of telephone and electronic monitoring equipment.*

7. I understand that I can expect telephone calls and unannounced visits to my residence by the service provider for the purpose of:

a) *inspecting and maintaining the monitoring equipment;*
b) *checking my whereabouts in the case of a violation being reported on the central monitoring computer.*

8. I agree not to attach an answering machine or any other device to the electronic monitoring equipment.

9. I agree to provide a continuous supply of electricity for the monitoring equipment.

10. Where a telephone service already exists in my name at my residence, I authorise the service provider, on behalf of the Home Office, to arrange for variations to my existing telephone service and/or equipment hire contracts if required, at no additional cost to me.

I understand all of these rules and that non-compliance with any of them may result in my arrest for being in breach of my bail condition.

Signature of Defendant .... Date ....

Signature of Service
Provider's representative .... Date .... **Issue** ***D***

References

Ball, R. A., Huff, C. R. and Lilly, J.R. (1988). *House Arrest and Correctional Policy: doing time at home*. Newbury Park, Ca: Sage.

Baumer, T. L. and Mendelsohn, R.I. (1990). *Final Report. The Electronic Monitoring of Non-Violent Convicted Felons: an experiment in home detention*. Indianapolis: School of Public and Environmental Affairs, Indiana University.

Berry, B. (1985). 'Electronic jails: a new criminal justice concern'. *Justice Quarterly*, 2, pp. 1–22.

Bureau of Justice Assistance (1989). *Electronic Monitoring in Intensive Probation and Parole Programs*. Washington: Department of Justice.

Del Carmen R. V. and Vaughn, J. B. (1986). 'Legal issues in the use of electronic surveillance in probation'. *Federal Probation*, 50, pp. 60–69.

Friel, C. M., Vaughn, J. B. and Del Carmen, R. (1987). *Electronic Monitoring and Correctional Policy: the technology and its application*. Washington, DC: National Institute of Justice.

Gable, R. K. (1986) 'Application of personal telemonitoring to current problems in corrections'. *Journal of Criminal Justice*, 14, pp. 167–176.

Hatchett, P. (1987). *The Home Confinement Program: an appraisal of the electronic monitoring of offenders in Washtenaw County, Michigan.*

Home Office (1988a). *Prison Statistics England and Wales 1987*, Cm.547. London: HMSO.

Home Office (1988b). *Punishment, Custody and the Community*, Cm.424. London: HMSO.

Home Office (1990). *Statistical Bulletin 12/90: The prison population in 1989.* London: Home Office.

Houk, J. M. (1984). 'Electronic monitoring of probationers: a step towards big brother?'. *Golden Gate University Law Review*, 14, pp. 431–446.

House of Commons (1987). *Third Report from the Home Affairs Committee: State and use of prisons*, Vol. 1. London: HMSO.

Jolin, A. (1987). *Electronic Surveillance Program, Clackamas County Community Corrections, Oregon: Evaluation.*

Lilly, J. R. and Ball, R. A. (1987). 'A brief history of house arrest and electronic monitoring'. *Northern Kentucky Law Review*, 13, pp. 343–374.

Lilly, J. R., Ball R. A. and Wright, J. (1987). 'Home incarceration with electronic monitoring in Kenton County, Kentucky: an evaluation'. In McCarthy, B. R. (Ed.), *Intermediate Punishments: intensive supervision, home confinement and electronic surveillance*. New York: Willow Tree Press.

Lilly, J. R. and Wright, J. (1986). *Home Incarceration with Electronic Monitoring in Kenton County, Ky: Final report.*

Mair, G. (1988). *Bail and Probation Work: the ILPS temporary bail action project*. Research and Planning Unit Paper 46. London: Home Office.

Mendelsohn, R. I. and Baumer, T. L. (1987). 'Observations on electronically monitored home detention: details at eleven'. Paper presented at the Annual Meeting of the American Society of Criminology, Montreal, Quebec.

Phillpotts, G. J. O. and Lancucki, L. B. (1979). *Previous convictions, sentence and reconviction*. Home Office Research Study No. 53. London: HMSO.

Renzema, M. and Skelton, D. (1990). 'Trends in the use of electronic monitoring: 1989'. *Journal of Offender Monitoring*, 3(3), pp. 12–19.

Schmidt, A. (1986). 'Electronic monitors'. *Federal Probation*, 50, pp. 56–59.

Stone, C. (1988). *Bail Information for the Crown Prosecution Service*. London: Vera Institute of Justice.

Sullivan, P. and Alpert, G. P. (1986). 'Electronic monitoring devices: alternative sentences and punishment rationales'. Paper presented at the Annual Meeting of the American Society of Criminology, Atlanta, Georgia.

Publications

Titles already published for the Home Office

Studies in the Causes of Delinquency and the Treatment of Offenders (SCDTO)

1. Prediction methods in relation to borstal training. Hermann Mannheim and Leslie T. Wilkins. 1955. viii + 276pp. (11 340051 9).
2. *Time spent awaiting trial. Evelyn Gibson. 1960. v + 45pp. (34–368–2).
3. *Delinquent generations. Leslie T. Wilkins. 1960. iv + 20pp. (11 340053 5).
4. *Murder. Evelyn Gibson and S. Klein. 1961. iv + 44pp. (11 340054 3).
5. Persistent criminals. A study of all offenders liable to preventive detention in 1956. W. H. Hammond and Edna Chayen. 1963. ix + 237pp. (34–368–5).
6. *Some statistical and other numerical techniques for classifying individuals. P. McNaughton-Smith. 1965. v + 33pp. (34–368–6).
7. Probation research: a preliminary report. Part I. General outline of research. Part II. Study of Middlesex probation area (SOMPA). Steven Folkard, Kate Lyon, Margaret M. Carver and Erica O'Leary. 1966. vi + 58pp. (11 340374 7).
8. *Probation research: national study of probation. Trends and regional comparisons in probation (England and Wales). Hugh Barr and Erica O'Leary. 1966. vii + 51pp. (34–368–8).
9. *Probation research. A survey of group work in the probation service. Hugh Barr. 1966. vii + 94pp. (34–368–9).
10. *Types of delinquency and home background. A validation study of Hewitt and Jenkins' hypothesis. Elizabeth Field. 1967. vi + 21pp. (34–368–10).
11. *Studies of female offenders. No. 1—Girls of 16–20 years sentenced to borstal or detention centre training in 1963. No. 2—Women offenders in the Metropolitan Police District in March and April 1957. No. 3—A description of women in prison on January 1, 1965. Nancy Goodman and Jean Price. 1967. v + 78pp. (34–368–11).
12. *The use of the Jesness Inventory on a sample of British probationers. Martin Davies. 1967. iv + 20pp. (34–368–12).
13. *The Jesness Inventory: application to approved school boys. Joy Mott. 1969. iv + 27pp. (11 340063 2).

Home Office Research Studies (HORS)

1. *Workloads in children's departments. Eleanor Grey. 1969. vi + 75pp. (11 340101 9).
2. *Probationers in their social environment. A study of male probationers aged 17–20, together with an analysis of those reconvicted within twelve months. Martin Davies. 1969. vii + 204pp. (11 340102 7).
3. *Murder 1957 to 1968. A Home Office Statistical Division report on murder in England and Wales. Evelyn Gibson and S. Klein (with annex by the Scottish Home and Health Department on murder in Scotland). 1969. vi + 94pp. (11 340103 5).
4. Firearms in crime. A Home Office Statistical Division report on indictable offences involving firearms in England and Wales. A. D. Weatherhead and B. M. Robinson. 1970. viii + 39pp. (11 340104 3).
5. *Financial penalties and probation. Martin Davies. 1970. vii + 39pp. (11 340105 1).

---

* Out of Print

6. *Hostels for probationers. A Study of the aims, working and variations in effectiveness of male probation hostels with special reference to the influence of the environment on delinquency. Ian Sinclair. 1971. ix + 200pp. (11 340106 X).
7. *Prediction methods in criminology—including a prediction study of young men on probation. Frances H. Simon. 1971. xi + 234pp. (11 340107 8).
8. *Study of the juvenile liaison scheme in West Ham 1961–65. Marilyn Taylor. 1971. vi + 46pp. (11 340108 6).
9. *Explorations in after-care. I—After-care units in London, Liverpool and Manchester. Martin Silberman (Royal London Prisoners' Aid Society) and Brenda Chapman. II—After-care hostels receiving a Home Office grant. Ian Sinclair and David Snow (HORU). II—St. Martin of Tours House, Aryeh Leissner (National Bureau for Co-operation in Child Care). 1971. xi + 140pp. (11 340109 4).
10. A survey of adoption in Great Britain. Eleanor Grey in collaboration with Ronald M. Blunden. 1971. ix + 168pp. (11 340110 8).
11. *Thirteen-year-old approved school boys in 1962s. Elizabeth Field, W. H. Hammond and J. Tizard. 1971. ix + 46pp. (11 340111 6).
12. Absconding from approved schools. R. V. G. Clarke and D. N. Martin. 1971. vi + 146pp. (11 340112 4).
13. An experiment in personality assessment of young men remanded in custody. H. Sylvia Anthony. 1972. viii + 79pp. (11 340113 2).
14. *Girl offenders aged 17–20 years. I—Statistics relating to girl offenders aged 17–20 years from 1960 to 1970. II—Re-offending by girls released from borstal or detention centre training. III—The problems of girls released from borstal training during their period on after-care. Jean Davies and Nancy Goodman. 1972. v + 77pp. (11 340114 0).
15. *The controlled trial in institutional research—paradigm or pitfall for penal evaluators? R. V. G. Clarke and D. B. Cornish. 1972. v + 33pp. (11 340115 9).
16. *A survey of fine enforcement. Paul Softley. v + 65pp. (11 340116 7).
17. *An index of social environment—designed for use in social work menum research. Martin Davies. 1973. vi + 63pp. (11 340117 5).
18. *Social enquiry reports and the probation service. Martin Davies and Andrea Knopf. 1973. v + 49pp. (11 340118 3).
19. *Depression psychopathic personality and attempted suicide in a borstal sample. H. Sylvia Anthony. 1973. viii + 44pp. (0 11 340119 1).
20. *The use of bail and custody by London magistrates' courts before and after the Criminal Justice Act 1967. Frances Simon and Mollie Weatheritt. 1974. vi + 78pp. (0 11 340120 5).
21. *Social work in the environment. A study of one aspect of probation practice. Martin Davies, with Margaret Rayfield, Alaster Calder and Tony Fowles. 1974. ix + 151pp. (0 11 340121 3).
22. Social work in prison. An experiment in the use of extended contact with offenders. Margaret Shaw. 1974. viii + 154pp. (0 11 340122 1).
23. Delinquency amongst opiate users. Joy Mott and Marilyn Taylor. 1974. vi + 31pp. (0 11 340663 0).
24. IMPACT. Intensive matched probation and after-care treatment. Vol. I—The design of the probation experiment and an interim evaluation. M. S. Folkard, A. J. Fowles, B. C. McWilliams, W. McWilliams, D. D. Smith, D. E. Smith and G. R. Walmsley. 1974. v + 54pp. (0 11 340664 9).
25. The approved school experience. An account of boys' experiences of training under differing regimes of approved schools, with an attempt to evaluate the effectiveness of that training. Anne B. Dunlop. 1974. vii + 124pp. (0 11 340665 7).
26. *Absconding from open prisons. Charlotte Banks, Patricia Mayhew and R. J. Sapsford. 1975. viii + 89pp. (0 11 340666 5).
27. Driving while disqualified. Sue Kriefman. 1975. vi + 136pp. (0 11 340667 3).
28. Some male offenders' problems. I—Homeless offenders in Liverpool. W. McWilliams. II—Casework with short-term prisoners. Julie Holborn. 1975. x + 147pp. (0 11 340668 1).
29. *Community service orders. K. Pease, P. Durkin, I. Earnshaw, D. Payne and J. Thorpe. 1975. viii + 80pp. (0 11 340669 X).
30. Field Wing Bail Hostel: the first nine months. Frances Simon and Sheena Wilson. 1975. viii + 55pp. (0 11 340670 3).

---

* Out of Print

31. Homicide in England and Wales 1967–1971. Evelyn Gibson. 1975. iv+59pp. (0 11 340753 X).
32. Residential treatment and its effects on delinquency. D. B. Cornish and R. V. G. Clarke. 1975. vi+74pp. (0 11 340672 X).
33. Further studies of female offenders. Part A: Borstal girls eight years after release. Nancy Goodman, Elizabeth Maloney and Jean Davies. Part B: The sentencing of women at the London Higher Courts. Nancy Goodman, Paul Durkin and Janet Halton. Part C: Girls appearing before a juvenile court. Jean Davies. 1976. vi+114pp. (0 11 340673 8).
34. *Crime as opportunity. P. Mayhew, R. V. G. Clarke, A. Sturman and J. M. Hough. 1976. vii+36pp. (0 11 340674 6).
35. The effectiveness of sentencing: a review of the literature. S. R. Brody. 1976. v+89pp. (0 11 340675 4).
36. IMPACT. Intensive matched probation and after-care treatment. Vol. II—The results of the experiment. M. S. Folkard, D. E. Smith and D. D. 1976. xi+40pp. (0 11 340676 2).
37. Police cautioning in England and Wales. J. A. Ditchfield. 1976. v+31pp. (0 11 340677 0).
38. Parole in England and Wales. C. P. Nuttall, with E. E. Barnard, A. J. Fowles, A. Frost, W. H. Hammond, P. Mayhew, K. Pease, R. Tarling and M. J. Weatheritt. 1977. vi+90pp. (0 11 340678 9).
39. Community service assessed in 1976. K. Pease, S. Billingham and I. Earnshaw. 1977. vi+29pp. (0 11 340679 7).
40. Screen violence and film censorship: a review of research. Stephen Brody. 1977. vii+179pp. (0 11 340680 0).
41. *Absconding from borstals. Gloria K. Laycock. 1977. v+82pp. (0 11 340681 9).
42. Gambling: a review of the literatue and its implications for policy and research. D. B. Cornish. 1978. xii+284pp. (0 11 340682 7).
43. Compensation orders in magistrates' courts. Paul Softley. 1978. v+41pp. (0 11 340683 5).
44. Research in criminal justice. John Croft. 1978. iv+16pp. (0 11 340684 3).
45. Prison welfare: an account of an experiment at Liverpool. A. J. Fowles. 1978. v+34pp. (0 11 340685 1).
46. Fines in magistrates' courts. Paul Softley. 1978. v+42pp. (0 11 340686 X).
47. Tackling vandalism. R. V. G. Clarke (editor), F. J. Gladstone, A. Sturman and Sheena Wilson (contributors). 1978. vi+91pp. (0 11 340687 8).
48. Social inquiry reports: a survey. Jennifer Thorpe. 1979. vi+55pp. (0 11 340688 6).
49. Crime in public view. P. Mayhew, R. V. G. Clarke, J. N. Burrows, J. M. Hough and S. W. C. Winchester. 1979. v+36pp. (0 11 340689 4).
50. *Crime and the community. John Croft. 1979. v+16pp. (0 11 340690 8).
51. Life-sentence prisoners. David Smith (editor), Christopher Brown, Joan Worth, Roger Sapsford and Charlotte Banks (contributors). 1979. iv+51pp. (0 11 340691 6).
52. Hostels for offenders. Jane E. Andrews, with an appendix by Bill Sheppard. 1979. v+30pp. (0 11 340692 4).
53. Previous convictions, sentence and reconviction: a statistical study of a sample of 5,000 offenders convicted in January 1971. G. J. O. Phillpotts and L. B. Lancucki. 1979. v+55pp. (0 11 340693 2).
54. Sexual offences, consent and sentencing. Roy Walmsley and Karen White. 1979. vi+77pp. (0 11 340694 0).
55. Crime prevention and the police. John Burrows, Paul Ekblom and Kevin Heal. 1979. v+37pp. (0 11 340695 9).
56. Sentencing practice in magistrates' courts. Roger Tarling, with the assistance of Mollie Weatheritt. 1979. vii+54pp. (0 11 340696 7).
57. Crime and comparative research. John Croft. 1979. iv+16pp. (0 11 340697 5).
58. Race, crime and arrests. Philip Stevens and Carole F. Willis. 1979. v+69pp. (0 11 340698 3).
59. Research and criminal policy. John Croft. 1980. iv+14pp. (0 11 340699 1).
60. Junior attendance centres. Anne B. Dunlop. 1980. v+47pp. (0 11 340700 9).
61. Police interrogation: an observational study in four police stations. Paul Softley, with the assistance of David Brown, Bob Forde, George Mair and David Moxon. 1980. vii+67pp. (0 11 340701 7).
62. Co-ordinating crime prevention efforts. F. J. Gladstone. 1980. v+74pp. (0 11 340702 5).

---

* Out of Print

63. Crime prevention publicity: an assessment. D. Riley and P. Mayhew. 1980. v+47pp. (0 11 340703 3).
64. Taking offenders out of circulation. Stephen Brody and Roger Tarling. 1980. v+46pp. (0 11 340704 1).
65. *Alcoholism and social policy: are we on the right lines? Mary Tuck. 1980. v+30pp. (0 11 340705 X).
66. Persistent petty offenders. Suzan Fairhead. 1981. vi+78pp. (0 11 340706 8).
67. Crime control and the police. Pauline Morris and Kevin Heal. 1981. v+71pp. (0 11 340707 6).
68. Ethnic minorities in Britain: a study of trends in their position since 1961. Simon Field, George Mair, Tom Rees and Philip Stevens. 1981. v+48pp. (0 11 340708 4).
69. Managing criminological research. John Croft. 1981. iv+17pp. (0 11 340709 2).
70. Ethnic minorities, crime and policing: a survey of the experiences of West Indians and whites. Mary Tuck and Peter Southgate. 1981. iv+54pp. (0 11 340765 3).
71. Contested trials in magistrates' courts. Julie Vennard. 1982. v+32pp. (0 11 340766 1).
72. Public disorder: a review of research and a study in one inner city area. Simon Field and Peter Southgate. 1982. v+77pp. (0 11 340767 X).
73. Clearing up crime. John Burrows and Roger Tarling. 1982. vii+31pp. (0 11 340768 8).
74. Residential burglary: the limits of prevention. Stuart Winchester and Hilary Jackson. 1982. v+47pp. (0 11 340769 6).
75. Concerning crime. John Croft. 1982. iv+16pp. (0 11 340770 X).
76. The British Crime Survey: first report. Mike Hough and Pat Mayhew. 1983. v+62pp. (0 11 340786 6).
77. Contacts between police and public: findings from the British Crime Survey. Peter Southgate and Paul Ekblom. 1984. v+42pp. (0 11 34771 8).
78. Fear of crime in England and Wales. Michael Maxfield. 1984. v+57pp. (0 11 340772 6).
79. Crime and police effectiveness. Ronald V. Clarke and Mike Hough. 1984. iv+33pp. (0 11 340773 3).
80. The attitudes of ethnic minorities. Simon Field. 1984. v+49pp. (0 11 340774 2).
81. Victims of crime: the dimensions of risk. Michael Gottfredson. 1984. v+54pp. (0 11 340775 0).
82. The tape recording of police interviews with suspects: an interim report. Carole Willis. 1984. v+45pp. (0 11 340776 9).
83. Parental supervision and juvenile delinquency. David Riley and Margaret Shaw. 1985. v+90pp. (0 11 340799 8).
84. Adult prisons and prisoners in England and Wales 1970–1982: a review of the findings of social research. Joy Mott. 1985. vi+73pp. (0 11 340801 3).
85. Taking account of crime: key findings from the 1984 British Crime Survey. Mike Hough and Pat Mayhew. 1985. vi+115pp. (0 11 341810 2).
86. Implementing crime prevention measures. Tim Hope. 1985. vi+82pp. (0 11 340812 9).
87. Resettling refugees: the lessons of research. Simon Field. 1985. vi+66pp. (0 11 340815 3).
88. Investigating burglary: the measurement of police performance. John Burrows. vi+36pp. (0 11 340824 2).
89. Personal violence. Roy Walmsley. 1986. vi+87pp. (0 11 340827 7).
90. Police-public encounters. Peter Southgate. 1986. vi+150pp. (0 11 340834 X).
91. Grievance procedures in prisons. John Ditchfield and Claire Austin. 1986. vi+87pp. (0 11 340839 0).
92. The effectiveness of the Forensic Science Service. Malcolm Ramsay. 1987. v+100pp. (0 11 340842 0).
93. The police complaints procedure: a survey of complainant's views. David Brown. 1987. v+98pp. (0 11 340853 6).
94. The validity of the reconviction prediction score. Denis Ward. 1987. vi+46. (0 11 340882 X).
95. Economic aspects of the illicit drug market enforcement policies in the United Kingdom. Adam Wagstaff and Alan Maynard. 1988. vii+156pp. (0 11 340883 8).
96. Schools, disruptive behaviour and delinquency: a review of literature. John Graham. 1988. v+70pp. (0 11 340887 0).

* Out of Print

97. The tape recording of police interviews with suspects: a second interim report. Carole Willis, John Macleod and Peter Naish. 1988. vii + 97pp. (0 11 340890 0).
98. Triable-either-way cases: Crown Court or magistrates' court. David Riley and Julie Vennard. 1988. v + 52pp. (0 11 340891 9).
99. Directing patrol work: a study of uniformed policing. John Burrows and Helen Lewis. 1988. v + 66pp. (0 11 340891 9).
100. Probation day centres. George Mair. 1988. v + 44pp. (0 11 340894 3).
101. Amusement machines: dependency and delinquency. John Graham. 1988. v + 48pp. (0 11 340895 1).
102. The use and enforcement of compensation orders in magistrates' courts. Tim Newburn. 1988. v + 49pp. (0 11 340896 X).
103. Sentencing practice in the Crown Court. David Moxon. 1988. v + 90pp. (0 11 340902 8).
104. Detention at the police station under the Police and Criminal Evidence Act 1984. David Brown. 1988. v + 88pp. (0 11 340908 7).
105. Changes in rape offences and sentencing. Charles Lloyd and Roy Walmsley. 1989. vi + 53pp. (0 11 340910 9).
106. Concers about rape. Lorna Smith. 1989. v + 48pp. (0 11 340911 7).
107. Domestic violence. Lorna Smith. 1989. v + 132pp. (0 11 340925 7).
108. Drinking and disorder: a study of non-metropolitan violence. Mary Tuck. 1989. v + 111pp. (0 11 340926 5).
109. Special security units. Roy Walmsley. 1989. v + 114pp. (0 11 340961 3).
110. Pre-trial delay: the implications of time limits. Patricia Morgan and Julie Vennard. 1989. v + 66pp. (0 11 340964 8).
111. The 1988 British Crime Survey. Pay Mayhew, David Elliott and Lizanne Dowds. 1989. v + 133pp. (0 11 340965 6).
112. The settlement of claims at the Criminal Injuries Compensation Board. Tim Newburn. 1989. v + 40pp. (0 11 340967 2).
113. Race, community groups and service delivery. Hilary Jackson and Simon Field. 1989. v + 62pp. (0 11 340972 9).
114. Money payment supervision orders: probation policy and practice. George Mair and Charles Lloyd. 1989. v + 40pp. (0 11 340971 0).
115. Suicide and self-injury in prison: a literature review. Charles Lloyd. 1990. v + 69pp. (0 11 3409745 5).
116. Keeping in Touch: police-victim communication in two areas. Tim Newburn and Susan Merry. 1990. v + 52pp. (0 11 340974 5).
117. The police and public in England and Wales: a British Crime Survey report. Wesley G. Skogan. 1990. vi + 74pp. (0 11 340995 8).
118. Control in prisons: a review of the literature. John Ditchfield. 1990. (0 11 340996 6).
119. Trends in crime and their interpretation: a study of post war England and Wales. Simon Field. 1990. v + 90pp. (0 11 340994 X).

ALSO

Designing out crime. R. V. G. Clarke and P. Mayhew (editors). 1980. viii + 186pp. (0 11 340732 7).
(This book collects, with an introduction, studies that were originally published in HORS 34, 47, 49, 55, 62 and 63 and which are illustrative of the 'situational' approach to crime prevention.)

Policing today. Kevin Heal, Roger Tarling and John Burrows (editors). v + 181pp. (0 11 340800 5).
This book brings together twelve separate studies on police matters produced during the last few years by the Unit. The collection records some relatively little known contributions to the debate on policing.)

Managing Criminal Justice: a collection of papers. David Moxon (ed.). 1985. vi + 222pp. (0 11 340811 0).
(This book brings together a number of studies bearing on the management of the criminal justice system. It includes papers by social scientists and operational researchers working within the Research and Planning Unit, and academic researchers who have studied particular aspects of the criminal process.)

Situational Crime Prevention: from theory into practice. Kevin Heal and Gloria Laycock (editors). 1986. vii + 166pp. (0 11 340826 9).
(Following the publication of *Designing Out Crime*, further research has been completed on the theoretical background to crime prevention. In drawing this work together this book sets down some of the theoretical concerns and discusses the emerging practical issues. It includes contributions by Unit staff as well as academics from this country and abroad.)
Communities and crime reduction. Tim Hope and Margaret Shaw (eds.). 1988. vii + 311pp. (11 340892 7).
(The central theme of this book is the possibility of preventing crime by building upon the resources of local communities and of active citizens. The specially commissioned chapters, by distinguished international authors, review contemporary research and policy on community crime prevention.)
New directions in police training. Peter Southgate (ed). 1988. xi + 256pp. (11 340889 7).
(Training is central to the development of the police role, and particular thought and effort now go into making it more responsive to current needs—in order to produce police officers who are both effective and sensitive in their dealing with the public. This book illustrates some of the thinking and research behind these developments.)

The above HMSO publications can be purchased from Government Bookshops or through booksellers.

The following Home Office research publications are available on request from the Home Office Research and Planning Unit, 50 Queen Anne's Gate, London SW1H 9AT.

Research Unit Papers (RUP)

1. Uniformed police work and management technology. J. M. Hough. 1980.
2. Supplementary information on sexual offences and sentencing. Roy Walmsley and Karen White. 1980.
3. Board of visitor adjudications. David Smith, Claire Austin and John Ditchfield. 1981.
4. Day centres and probation. Suzan Fairhead, with the assistance of J. Wilkinson-Grey. 1981.

Research and Planning Unit Papers (RPUP)

5. Ethnic minorities and complaints against the police. Philip Stevens and Carole Willis. 1982.
6. *Crime and public housing. Mike Hough and Pat Mayhew (editors). 1982.
7. *Abstracts of race relations research. George Mair and Philip Stevens (editors). 1982.
8. Police probationer training in race relations. Peter Southgate. 1982.
9. *The police response to calls from the public. Paul Ekblom and Kevin Heal. 1982.
10. City Centre crime: a situational approach to prevention. Malcom Ramsay. 1982.
11. Burglary in schools: the prospects for prevention. Tim Hope. 1982.
12. *Fine enforcement. Paul Softley and David Moxon. 1982.
13. Vietnamese refugees. Peter Jones. 1982.
14. Community resources for victims of crime. Karen Williams. 1983.
15. The use, effectiveness and impact of police stop and search powers. Carole Willis. 1983.
16. Acquittal rates. Sid Butler. 1983.
17. Criminal justice comparisons: the case of Scotland and England and Wales. Lorna J. F. Smith. 1983.
18. Time taken to deal with juveniles under criminal proceedings. Catherine Frankenburg and Roger Tarling. 1983.
19. Civilian review of complaints against the police: a survey of the United States literature. David C. Brown. 1983.
20. Police action on motoring offences. David Riley. 1983.

---

* Out of Print

21. *Diverting drunks from the criminal justice system. Sue Kinglsey and George Mair. 1983.
22. The staff resource implications of an independent prosecution system. Peter R. Jones. 1983.
23. Reducing the prison population: an exploratory study in Hampshire. David Smith, Bill Sheppard, George Mair, Karen Williams. 1984.
24. Criminal justice system model: magistrates' courts sub-model. Susan Rice. 1984.
25. Measures of police effectiveness and efficiency. Ian Sinclair and Clive Miller. 1984.
26. Punishment practice by prison Boards of Visitors. Susan Iles, Adrienne Connors, Chris May, Joy Mott. 1984.
27. *Reparation, conciliation and mediation: current projects and plans in England and Wales. Tony Marshall. 1984.
28. Magistrates' domestic courts: new perspectives. Tony Marshall (editor). 1984.
29. Racism awareness training for the police. Peter Southgate. 1984.
30. Community constables: a study of a policing initiative. David Brown and Susan Iles. 1985.
31. Recruiting volunteers. Hilary Jackson. 1985.
32. Juvenile sentencing: is there a tariff? David Moxon, Peter Jones, Roger Tarling. 1985.
33. Bringing people together: mediation and reparation projects in Great Britain. Tony Marshall and Martin Walpole. 1985.
34. Remands in the absence of the accused. Chris May. 1985.
35. Modelling the criminal justice system. Patricia M. Morgan. 1985.
36. The criminal justice system model: the flow model. Hugh Pullinger. 1986.
37. Burglary: police actions and victim views. John Burrows. 1986.
38. Unlocking community resources: four experimental government small grant schemes. Hilary Jackson. 1986.
39. The cost of discriminating: a review of the literature. Shirley Dex. 1986.
40. Waiting for Crown Court trial: the remand population. Rachel Pearce. 1987.
41. Children's evidence the need for corroboration. Carol Hedderman. 1987
42. A preliminary study of victim offender mediation and reparation schemes in England & Wales. Gwynn Davis, Jacky Boucherat, David Watson, Adrian Thatcher (Consultant). 1987.
43. Explaining fear of crime: evidence from the 1984 British Crime Survey. Michael Maxfield. 1987.
44. Judgements of crime seriousness: evidence from the 1984 British Crime Survey. Ken Pease. 1988.
45. Waiting time on the day in magistrates' courts: a review of case listings practises. David Moxon and Roger Tarling (editors). 1988.
46. Bail and probation work: the ILPS temporary bail action project. George Mair. 1988.
47. Police work and manpower allocation. Roger Tarling. 1988.
48. Computers in the courtroom. Carol Hedderman. 1988.
49. Data interchange between magistrates' courts and other agencies. Carol Hedderman. 1988.
50. Bail and probation work II: the use of London probation/bail hostels for bailees. Helen Lewis and George Mair. 1989.
51. The role and function of police community liaison officers. Susan V. Phillips and Raymond Cochrane. 1989.
52. Insuring against burglary losses. Helen Lewis. 1989.
53. Remand decisions in Brighton and Bournemeth. Patricia Morgan and Rachel Pearce. 1989.
54. Racially motivated incidents reported to the police. Jayne Seagrave. 1989.
55. Review of research on re-offending of mentally disordered offenders. David J. Murray. 1990.
56. Risk prediction and probation: papers from a Research and Planning Unit workshop. George Mair (editor). 1990.
57. Household fires: findings from the British Crime Survey 1988. Chris May. 1990.
58. Home Office funding of victim support schemes—money well spent? Justin Russell. 1990.

---

* Out of Print

Research Bulletin

The Research Bulletin is published twice a year and consists mainly of short articles relating to projects which are part of the Home Office Research and Planning Unit's research programme.

Printed in the United Kingdom for HMSO
Dd293607 10/90 C14 G443 10170